SHERLOCK HOLMES AND MUCH MORE

Courtesy of The Stowe-Day Foundation

William Gillette as Sherlock Holmes

SHERLOCK HOLMES
AND MUCH MORE

or some of the facts about William Gillette

BY

DORIS E. COOK

The Connecticut Historical Society

1970

Copyright 1970 by The Connecticut Historical Society
Hartford, Connecticut
Printed by Connecticut Printers, Incorporated
Designed by Asher T. Applegate

Foreword

WILLIAM GILLETTE, I am sure, would have discouraged biographers, had any sought his cooperation. Yet, as he welcomed enthusiastic audiences, I like to think that he would welcome appreciation of, and pleasure in, his life and work.

In the 1940's, the Librarian of the State of Connecticut, Mr. James Brewster, brought from Gillette Castle to the Connecticut State Library approximately half of William Gillette's library and a dozen or more of the water color paintings of the Connecticut artist, Amelia M. Watson, whose work Gillette so admired. These two collections were the origin of my interest in William Gillette.

There are difficulties for a biographer of Gillette. He left no memoirs, being too busy still living. As of this time, the writer wishing to reconstruct his life must work with secondary sources and with a comparatively small number of letters scattered in libraries, collections, or private hands all across the country. Probably the most humanly revealing of these are the Gillette letters in the James Beecher Collection at the Schlesinger Library at Radcliffe College, the Gillette, Warner, and Hooker letters at the Stowe-Day Foundation, Hartford, and the Gillette letters to "Dr." Fuller, which are at The Connecticut Historical Society in Hartford.

I should like to express gratitude to The Connecticut Historical Society, Thompson R. Harlow, Director, and to the Stowe-Day Foundation, Joseph S. Van Why, Director, for making publication possible, and appreciation for the work of the late Mr. Brewster, of P. M. Stone, late of Waltham, Massachusetts, a Gillette and Sherlock Holmes enthusiast, who kept alive my interest and without whose date-filled articles I should have been unable to report Gillette's theatrical career, and to James Keddie, Jr., of Wellesley Hills, Massachusetts, who in many ways has taken "P. M.'s" place.

Grateful thanks and appreciation are due to William L. Warren, former Director of the Stowe-Day Foundation, and to its staff, to Joseph K. Hooker, of Hartford, Gillette's cousin, to Dr. Glenn Weaver of Trinity College and to Miss Frances A. Hoxie and Miss Phyllis Kihn of The Connecticut Historical Society for suggestions as to the final form of the manuscript, and finally to many colleagues and friends, of whom two in particular, Miss Helen C. Bragdon of the Flat Rock, North Carolina, Playhouse, and Miss Frances Davenport of the Connecticut State Library, have shared enthusiasm, disenchantment, and reappraisal, and have helped by listening over many years.

It has been fun; of that, I am sure, William Gillette would approve.

DORIS E. COOK

Contents

		Page
CHAPTER I	Early Years in Hartford, Conn.	3
CHAPTER II	Getting Started in the Theatre	10
CHAPTER III	First Successes and Marriage	17
CHAPTER IV	Troubled Years	32
CHAPTER V	Acting Again in His Own Plays	40
CHAPTER VI	Sherlock Holmes, Etc.	48
CHAPTER VII	More Acting and a New Play	59
CHAPTER VIII	"Retirement"	67
CHAPTER IX	Honors and Last Farewells	79
CHAPTER X	As They Saw Him and As He Was	93
NOTES		103

Illustrations

FRONTISPIECE: William Gillette as Sherlock Holmes	*ii*
Will Gillette	*11*
Helen (Nickles) Gillette	*18*
Will Gillette as Shylock, 1875	*22*
Scene from "Held by the Enemy"	*27*
Scene from "The Private Secretary"	*29*
Scene from "The Private Secretary"	*34*
Attic Room, Forest Street house	*37*
Will Gillette in attic room, with steam engine he constructed as a boy	*37*
William Gillette in "Sherlock Holmes"	*49*
Scene from "Clarice"	*53*
Scene from "Diplomacy"	*57*
A Gillette letter	*60*
The "Aunt Polly"	*68*
Saloon of the "Aunt Polly"	*68*
Helen Hayes and William Gillette in "Dear Brutus"	*75*
The big fireplace, Gillette Castle	*80*
Gillette in the cab of one of his locomotives	*84*
Gillette with railroad engineers	*84*
Gillette Castle, Hadlyme	*89*
William Gillette	*94*

SHERLOCK HOLMES AND MUCH MORE

CHAPTER I

Early years in Hartford, Connecticut

As one of his Christmas presents in 1866, thirteen-year-old William H. Gillette received a book by Frank Bellew called *The Art of Amusing*.[1] Mr. Bellew's title-page bore the note: "A volume intended to amuse everybody and enable all to amuse everybody else; thus bringing about as near an approximation to the millenium as can be conveniently attained in the small compass of one small volume." The book contained instructions for games, tricks, puzzles, and charades, and suggestions for private theatricals, tableaux, and all sorts of parlor and family amusements. Susan L. Warner, the giver, wife of Charles Dudley Warner of the Nook Farm community in Hartford, chose well for her young friend. He had already begun, and indeed was to make a lifelong business of the art of amusing, not only himself, but other people—many of them.

Perhaps, at the start, it was in some ways a necessity for him. Will had two brothers and a sister, considerably older than he, but by this time he was virtually an only child. His oldest brother, Ashbell Frank, had gone West, and died in Sacramento, at the age of twenty-three, in 1859, when Will was six years old. In 1863, his older brother, Edward, went to Iowa at the age of twenty-three, and there engaged in farming, manufacturing, and some politicking; Will was then ten. The following September his sister, Eliza, became the wife of George Henry Warner, brother of Charles Dudley, in Hartford where she was to spend most of her life. In January 1865—Will was going on twelve—his second living older brother, Robert, died after the capture of Fort Fisher in North Carolina; he had been paymaster on the U.S. naval blockade vessel *Gettysburg*. Deaths and departures had left Will an only child of rather elderly parents; his mother was forty and his father forty-six when he was born in 1853. They were now, in 1866, fifty-two and fifty-eight. Little wonder that the boy thought, and later spoke of, his father as an "old gentleman".[2]

Will had playmates in Nook Farm and other parts of Hartford. There was his cousin Ned Hooker, two years younger, son of John and Isabella (Beecher) Hooker, nearby. There was a boy named French who lived on Asylum Street. H. W. French and Will had teamed up in a printing venture in June 1866, French apparently supplying the press and Will probably a good proportion of the copy. Their chief product was a journal titled "Hail Columbia". Contributors to the first issue were Will's father, the Honorable Francis Gillette, a Mr. Willard, Charles Dudley Warner, then associate editor of the *Hartford Evening Press,* and a Mrs. Warner of Cincinnati. The firm of Gillette and French set the subscription price at one dollar a year, and offered their services as job printers, willing to execute "all sorts of Plain Fancy and Ornamental PRINTING, CARDS OF ALL KINDS, LABELS, &", at their offices at 5 Forest St. and 342 Asylum St. To the October 1866 issue, a certain "L. H. S.", probably Hartford's "Sweet Singer", the poetess Lydia H. Sigourney, contributed a front-page story entitled "The Boy That Became a Traitor". The publisher-printers exchanged journals with other boys; "amateur journalism", as it was later called, was one of the leisure-time pursuits of bright boys and girls in the United States of the mid and later nineteenth century.

Besides stories, "Hail Columbia" ran news items, tongue-twisters, conundrums, and jokes, and was altogether a very creditable specimen of amateur journalism. After it had run for more than a year, with summer breaks, there appeared in Volume 2, Number 6, the issue of October 1867, the following notice:

> Dear Readers: This number ends the second volume of our paper, and we are forced to bid you goodbye for a while. We don't intend to continue through the winter so we stop now. Perhaps we shall resume again in spring, but we are not certain.
>
> We have tried hard to make Hail Columbia as interesting and attractive as possible, at no great profit to ourself.
>
> Like a salute of twelve guns, it has gone off and it has to be reloaded before it can shoot again. By the way, we hope we haven't killed anybody—unless it be copperhead snakes and such like.
>
> We should like to receive visitors at our office, where we do all kinds of printing as will be seen on last page.

Early Years in Hartford, Conn.

> To our Exchanges, we are sorry to be obliged to take leave of our Exchanges, but we must. We have enjoyed them exceedingly, and part with them against our will.
>
> We are very much indebted to our subscribers for having helped us so. We wouldn't have charged anything for our paper, only to cover the expense of carrying it on.[3]

The job printing set-up apparently was maintained, and came in handy for the boys on an occasion which the mature Gillette reported with evident relish to a *New York Times* interviewer in 1914. As he put it, he and a cousin about his own age were "awfully keen about the theatre and wanted to see everything that came along".[2] His parents, and indeed the Nook Farm adults generally, like the majority of respectable folk of that day, viewed the theatre with suspicion and alarm. For Shakespearean plays, however, some exceptions were made. Gillette told the reporter:

> My cousin and I wanted to see "The Colleen Bawn" [play by Dion Boucicault based on a novel by Gerald Griffin, *The Collegians,* founded on fact, and in effect, an Irish *American Tragedy*] which was coming to our town. And we thought it would be a splendid idea to make my father believe that that was one of Shakespeare's plays. If we could just do that we were sure it would be all right about going to see it. We found an old picture of Shakepeare writing at a desk, and on that we built our plot. For my cousin had a printing press and it was simple enough to print at the bottom of the picture the interesting legend 'William Shakespeare Writing "The Colleen Bawn" '. So I went to my father and told him all about the new Shakespeare play that was coming to our town. " 'The Colleen Bawn'?" repeated the old gentleman, "I don't remember that in Shakespeare's plays." And he got out his Shakespeare and showed me that it wasn't there. "Well," I said, "of course I don't know anything about it, but I found this picture." And I showed him 'William Shakespeare Writing "The Colleen Bawn" '. "H'm," he said, with a perfectly grave face, "if that is the case, I think you had both better go and see what it is like!" It was years before I knew that my father had let us go to the play because he really admired our sublime nerve![2]

The theatre, elders' disapproval notwithstanding, was establishing itself ever more securely as the years went by. In 1857, the year that Will's father, former United States Senator Francis Gillette, built his new house in Nook Farm, the City Theater opened in the old City Hall building at the corner of Market and Kinsley Streets,[4] a site to be occupied a century or so later by the theatre of the Hartford Stage Company. The City Theater ran one season, giving dramas only. Hartford's first modern theatre, Allyn Hall, was opened by Timothy Allyn in 1861 when Willie Gillette was eight; it occupied the top floor of a new building on Asylum Street west of the Allyn Hotel. Dramas, minstrels, operas, and lectures were offered; seats were removable and all the big balls were held there.[4] Eight years later in 1869, Hartford's first large theatre, Roberts Opera House, was built, bringing to the town all the leading plays, actors, operas, and minstrels. It was here, very probably, that Will and Ned managed to see "The Colleen Bawn" when the Boucicaults brought it to Hartford in March 1873.[5]

On the final day of the year 1869, Ned Hooker sent a message to Robert Allen in a letter written by his mother, Isabella, that his neighbor, Will Gillette, in the summer had made a small steam engine which would turn a wheel, and that "now he had a miniature theatre with images that dance (with the aid of thread) and sing (by the aid of his voice) and act characters".[6]

Otis Skinner, five years younger than Will Gillette, and like Gillette a future actor, was about this time toiling away at a commission house job in Hartford and feeling "the need to act as a race horse feels the need to run. He organized a youthful company of amateurs, among them William Gillette, whom he had known at Brown . . . School. Gillette was older than the rest of them, and his chief interest at the time was in puppets. However, he did allow the group to put on a couple of their plays in the loft of his family's carriage house . . . ."[7]

In a miniature theatre, with puppets performing as he willed and what he willed, the young Gillette prefigured his future theatrical career, the part of it, that is, which lay nearest his personal schemes and dreams.

Meantime, as a lad of seventeen, he sought favored amusement of another sort. His Aunt Isabella Hooker wrote Robert Allen that Ned (her son) and Will Gillette were planning some inexpensive trip for their vacation.[6] Will had probably just completed his freshman year at Hartford Public High School; vacation was in June.

Early Years in Hartford, Conn.

Hartford Public High School in the 1870's had two principal departments of study, the Classical and the English. Will Gillette started out in the Classical, but transferred to the English Department in June 1871 at the beginning of his junior year. Already, at eighteen—probably long before that—he had decided what he wanted to do. Report cards were formidable in the 1870's. Grades in scholarship, attendance, and deportment for each student in a class were printed, so that anyone might see at a glance what sort of record Will Gillette had made in, say, the month of March 1870; in fact, he had an average of 9.8 in scholarship and 10 in attendance and deportment. Except for three minor lapses in his freshman year, Will had a nearly perfect record in attendance and deportment. In scholarship he ranked high, apart from a slump at the beginning of his sophomore year. With the transfer to the English Department, his grades went back to the high 90's and 100's and so continued.[8]

High school offered opportunities to a would-be actor, and Will took advantage of them. On April 8, 1872, he delivered a declamation entitled "Cassius Inciting Brutus Against Caesar". There were elocution contests; these he described to a *New York Times* reporter many years later, indicating as he did so that his individual style of speaking had been worked out in response to a suggestion made by his father. He said:

> I had a taciturn old father who thought a good deal and didn't always tell what he thought. I could make out pretty often what was in his mind, and I always wanted to know, because I had so much respect for his opinion, and I wanted him to think well of me.
>
> Well, it was my next-to-the last year in high school, and I went in for the elocution contests. I always did. I liked them. You know the kind? The boys recited orations, and things like that; the girls read selections. And there were prizes. This year I chose a part of Daniel Webster's reply to Hayne—the famous reply that is said to have really killed Hayne, you know. I had worked very hard on it, and I did as well as I could, and I won the first prize... The next year I chose another speech of Webster's for my part in the elocution contest—and someone else got the prize. They said I didn't know my lines! [This time Will had delivered them in accordance with his father's suggestion.] I think of that scene with my father to this day. I think of it when I'm playing and when I'm studying a part and when I try to say something about the development of acting

in the last forty years. That old New England gentleman had the idea that has come to be the controlling idea on the stage today. . . The idea is that we are not reciting literature—not reciting anything that has ever been written or said before; we are talking, saying the first things that come into our heads, thinking them out as we say them, hesitating and wondering and sometimes blundering over it all. That is the way to recite Webster's speeches; it is the way to play Shakespeare; it is the way to do everything on the stage.[9]

William Gillette's manner of speaking on the stage, developed along these lines, made him one of the first American actors to speak rather than declaim his roles. It made him as well one of the first exponents of the modern technique of underacting.

April 1873 was graduation time, occasion for Class Day and Anniversary Exercises. For Class Day on April 3, Will contributed the text of one of four songs; his was sung to the tune of "The Battle Cry of Freedom" and the first verse ran:

> The High School had a jolly class
> Its fleece was not like snow
> And everywhere the High School went
> This Class was sure to go.

He also delivered the Class Prophecy.

Graduation exercises lasted for two days, beginning each morning at 10 A.M. On the first day, April 24, the program of anniversary exercises consisted of prize readings and declamations. Will delivered a selection from "Julius Caesar". On the following day, as part of the graduation exercises, W. H. Gillette's address, "Opposition", was noted in one of the local papers as "the best effort of the day" and "was long and loudly applauded".[10] W. H. Gillette was also on the Roll of Honor.

On June 11, 1873, Will went for a hiking vacation, recording it thus in the first of a two-volume set of Milton's *Poetical Works:* "Found in Book Case and taken on a 'Conn. Western Tramp' June 11th, 1873 By W. H. Gillette—Hartford—Conn."[11]

During his years of study at "H. P. H. S.", Will had not put aside the study of the art of amusing. Otis Skinner, who was a freshman at Hartford

Early Years in Hartford, Conn. 9

Public High School when Gillette was a senior, tells in *Footlights and Spotlights* of Will's "enacting humorous pieces of his own composition at class recitals in something of the dry manner which became a characteristic in his play 'The Private Secretary' ".[12]

Will almost certainly saw Edward Sothern as Lord Dundreary in "Our American Cousin" when it played Roberts Opera House in January 1872. What the *Hartford Times* referred to as the role's "patchwork of comic characteristics"[13] was something the aspiring actor could and did set himself to copy. In March 1873, a sociable was given by residents of Glenwood, a district in Hartford, the proceeds to be used to furnish a new chapel. The affair was held in the hall over Cushman's new factory on Sigourney Street. W. H. Gillette appeared in an imitation of Sothern as "Lord Dundreary", and the entertainment concluded with a one-act farce written by Will Gillette, entitled "Bullywingle the Beloved".[14]

At the end of 1873, and again in the first part of 1874, Hartford offered a much different kind of theatre. Tommaso Salvini, the great Italian actor, was making an American tour. Though Will bought copies of "The Gladiator", "Samson", and "Othello", in the texts prepared especially for the tour, there is a question whether he was in Hartford for the performances of "The Gladiator" on December 5, 1873 and of "Othello" on May 15, 1874, both at Roberts Opera House. Salvini's appearance and address were impressive. The *Hartford Courant* reported after "The Gladiator": "His physique is simply superb. He is a magnificent man." But superb and magnificent, "supreme interpreter of Shakespeare"[15] though he was, the young William Gillette saw no real image of his future acting self in Salvini, and felt no impulse to imitate or copy him.

CHAPTER II

Getting started in the theatre

Where was Will Gillette in the fall of 1873? His younger Nook Farm friend, Dick Burton, was to write years later that he, Gillette, disappeared just when it was time to go to college.[1] And indeed he would have been expected to go to college. He was a descendant of some of the first families of Connecticut whose men had been prominent in public life.[2] His father had been Phi Beta Kappa and valedictorian of the class of 1829 at Yale, briefly a United States Senator in 1854–55, and keenly interested in education, abolition, and other issues of the day. Will himself had made a fine record in high school.

Yet something had been at work in young William H. Gillette, a something that drew him away from the pleasant, ordered life of Nook Farm. At an age when many young men still do not know what will be their business in life, Will knew, somehow knew the most direct route to it, and took it even though that meant leaving familiar scenes and faces. It has been put that he ran away, but a more plausible story is that he left with the blessing of the father who had allowed him to see "The Colleen Bawn" and had told him how he thought an oration should be delivered.

At twenty Will Gillette had gone away to learn to be an actor, and was serving the beginning of a long apprenticeship, first at the Grand Opera House in St. Louis and at Ben De Bar's St. Charles Theatre in New Orleans.[3] The *St. Louis Daily Globe* of March 9, 1930[4] recalled that Gillette had his first speaking role with the De Bar company in St. Louis, supporting Lawrence Barrett who was touring in a repertory of classic and romantic plays of the old school, such as "Richelieu", "Hamlet", "Julius Caesar", "The Duke's Motto", and "Rosedale". The man who gave Gillette his first acting opportunity in St. Louis was William Seymour, distinguished actor of the nineteenth and early twentieth centuries.

Will told the *New York Times* reporter in 1914 that he could not in those early apprentice days act as he chose. "They wouldn't let me", he said. "I began very humbly indeed, in stock, and if I had tried to be nat-

10

Courtesy of Doris E. Cook

Will Gillette

ural, I'd have lost my position. My business then was to learn the tricks of the stage. We had our tragic walk, our proper comedy face, our correct and dreadful laugh, our carefully learned gestures, our shrieks and outcries and our stilted voices. We were to hope for success in so far as we mastered these rules and tricks and put force and personal 'vigor' into our execution of them."[5]

In Nook Farm, a neighbor of the Gillettes had been engaged in various activities which were to benefit Will Gillette. The neighbor, Mark Twain, had written a novel in 1873 in collaboration with Charles Dudley Warner. *The Gilded Age* had been very popular. In the summer of 1874, Mark heard that a California writer named Densmore was producing a play based on the novel. Mark himself had already planned to write such a play, and had taken out dramatic copyright. His first move now was to stop the California production and write the playwright; in the end he bought the California play. Then he rewrote it, enlarging upon the character of Colonel Sellers. John T. Raymond, who had been acting in the play, came East and signed a contract for production. The play was a great success.[6] Will Gillette, thanks to Mark, had a small role in "The Gilded Age" in the fall of 1874, and appeared with the company when it finally came to Hartford for performances on January 11 and 12, 1875. The *Hartford Courant* story of January 11 announced that "the theater-going public of Hartford, after waiting about four months for the termination of the run of 'The Gilded Age' at the Park Theater in New York, [would] have an opportunity of witnessing it at the Opera House" that evening.[7] Next morning's *Courant* reported that a magnificent audience had filled the Opera House to witness Mark Twain's first and only drama, based on *The Gilded Age*.[8] According to a biographer of Twain, "Raymond had reached the perfection of his art, by that time, and the townsmen of Mark Twain saw the play and the actor at their best. Kate Field played the part of Hawkins; there was a Hartford girl in the company, also a Hartford young man . . . ."[9]

Were there any Nook Farmers in the audience? This seems not to have been recorded. It *is* on record that in April following this January performance, Will's father, at the funeral of a Dr. Eldredge, a classmate, spoke to the Reverend Joseph Twichell about Will's choice of a calling, asking his opinion of it. The minister's answer was that though he would

Getting Started in the Theatre 13

not have chosen it, yet as Will had done so, he did not feel like being shocked or apprehensive.[10]

Mark knew that Hartford would think he was on dangerous ground in entering the theatrical world, and in bringing the Nook Farm group to it, he proceeded cautiously. Two good performances in January warranted a return, and this took place on May 6 and was duly reported in the *Courant* the next morning: " 'Col. Sellers' was repeated at the Opera House last evening, before a good-sized audience . . . The supporting company is essentially the same as when it last appeared here, but this time for some reason it comes announced as 'the company from the Globe Theater, Boston!' The troupe, however, it may be said, has talent enough to travel on its own merits. Among its members is Mr. Wm. H. Gillette of this city. He has been sometime traveling with Mr. Raymond, and assumed the part of Counsel for the Defense in the trial scene very creditably."[11] This was an advancement for Will who had earlier had the role of foreman of the jury, with only two or four words: "Not Guilty" or "We have—not guilty".

Will continued his apprenticeship with Raymond's company at the Globe Theatre in Boston through the rest of 1875 and the first half of 1876. His first important stage engagement was in "Faint Heart Ne'er Won Fair Lady", in the role of Guzman. In November 1875 he supported Raymond in "The Gilded Age" and played a wide variety of roles during the season: Lord Kootoo in "King Turko", Longford in "My Precious Betsey", Malcolm in "Macbeth", Montano in "Othello", Benvolio in "Romeo and Juliet", Markham in "Still Waters Run Deep", Master Wilford in "The Hunchback", Capt. Collins in "Around the World in Eighty Days", Mr. Buffler in "Married in Haste", Philippe in "La Tour de Nesle", Garnier in "Retribution", Gabriel in "Guy Mannering", the Duke of Suffolk in "A Crown of Thorns", Lord Milton in "The Marble Heart", Rosencranz in "Hamlet", Hortensio in "Katherine and Petruchio", Archambent in "The Child of the Regiment", the Admiral in "Black-Eyed Susan", and Prince Florian in "Broken Hearts". The *Boston Evening Transcript* of February 3, 1876 gave Gillette one of his first press notices: " 'Broken Hearts' and 'Tom Cobb' were restored to the boards last night, with Mr. W. H. Gillette very competently filling the part of Mr. Murdock, who is still seriously ill . . . ."[12]

During his year in Boston, Will submitted himself to the professors. This was his only truly formal education following high school.[13] He attended Boston University's Monroe School of Oratory for the one year on the junior class level; the full course leading to the "Diploma of Graduation" required two years. Students worked on "Culture of the Speaking Voice, Articulation, Orthoepy [science of pronunciation], Expressive Reading, Declamation, Gesture, Oratorical Action, and the Dramatic Art", and attended lectures on "English Literature, Logic, and Rhetoric, with occasional Dramatic Reading, also lectures on Diseases and Hygiene of the Voice, Laryngoscopy, Acoustics, Aesthetics, and other important subjects".[14] Gillette may have been thinking of the curriculum at Monroe, as well as his early experiences in the theatre, when he told the 1914 *New York Times* reporter of the older methods of acting.

September 1876 found Will heading West for two years with McCauley's Stock Company, in Cincinnati and Louisville, where some of the plays were Howard Bronson's "Saratoga; or, 'Pistols for Seven' ", Maria Lovell's "Ingomar, the Barbarian", Milman's "Fazio; or, the Italian Wife", Sheil's "Evadne; or, the Statue", Tom Taylor's "The Ticket-of-Leave Man", Almar's "Oliver Twist", Haines's "The French Spy", Milner's "Mazeppa; or, The Wild Horse of Tartary", Suter's "The Lost Child", Buckstone's "Married Life", Kotzebue's "The Stranger", Thomas Noon Talfourd's "Ion", "The Toodles", Colman's "Heir at Law" and "The Poor Gentleman", and John Howard Payne's "Brutus; or, The Fall of Tarquin". There was some Shakespeare now and then, and classics such as Goldsmith's "She Stoops to Conquer".[15]

On June 4, 1877, the *Hartford Courant* carried on its front page under "Amusements", the following ad:

Seminary Hall, Pratt St.
Tuesday Evening, June 5, 1877
Costume Impersonations
Comic Character Sketches!
Humorous Selections
Given By
W. H. Gillette
Late of the Theatres in New York, Boston, Cincinnati

> Louisville, New Orleans, and other cities.
> Imitation in Characteristic Scenes of
> Edwin Booth, Lawrence Barrett,
> John T. Raymond, Charles Fechter
> Stuart Robson, E. A. Sothern, etc.
> Admission 35 cents   Children 25 cents
> For sale at Brown & Gross's bookstore

According to the *Hartford Courant* report of June 6, headed "Mr. Gillette's Entertainment", there had been a full house with many standees. For Gillette's first major appearance in his native city, many had come out of curiosity. The audience adjudged his performance a "marked success", showing itself by frequent applause and laughter to be thoroughly entertained from beginning to end. The program was varied, running from tragedy to comedy and farce. One of the most popular pieces was a composition of Gillette's own, the supposed address of a bashful and conceited young man to a Sunday School. Equally successful was an imitation of Mark Twain in "The Jumping Frog", so well done that Mr. Clemens, who was in the audience, could have believed himself on the stage. There were contrasting interpretations of Hamlet in the styles of Fechter and Booth. Imitations of Solon Shingle and Lord Dundreary were excellent, and "convulsed the audience". The reviewer stated that Gillette's stage bearing was good, his elocution excellent, and that he showed promise of becoming an actor of mark and character. With his fine presence, good voice, keen sense of humor, and facility in both serious and comic roles, he predicted for him the attainment of a high place in his profession.[16]

After a fall season in Cincinnati and Louisville,[15] Will's presence in Hartford was necessitated for much of 1878 and 1879 by the ill-health, illness, and death of his father. Francis Gillette died on September 30, 1879. About two and a half weeks later, Miss Kate Claxton, well-known actress of the day, brought her company to Hartford. Her second offering, a Saturday matinee performance of "The Two Orphans", was presented as a benefit and a starring vehicle for W. H. Gillette. The *Hartford Times* reported that Miss Claxton's "support was good, more especially the beneficiary of the performance, Mr. Gillette. He played the gallant, young cavalier (the Chevalier de Vaudrey) with much spirit, with a tender expression of sentiment, and with courtly manners. It must have proved a gratification to all who knew him. Undoubtedly, his advance on the stage has been rapid, but then he had very good talents to begin with."[17]

Miss Claxton's motive for putting on a benefit for Gillette may have been sympathy with his personal, and possibly financial, problems, and an altruistic wish to bring the young and promising performer into public view again after what appears to have been an almost complete absence from the stage for approximately a year and nine months.

CHAPTER III

First successes and marriage

Gillette's real desire was to write, direct, and act in, his own plays. This triple command position would give him exactly the combination of responsibility and independence he wanted.

The time at home in 1878 and 1879 during his father's illness afforded the leisure he needed for completing and revising his first play. Hartford residents found on the first page of their *Courant*s for January 9, 1880, under the heading "Amusements", this ad:

Roberts Opera House
WILL GILLETTE
In his most Comical Character Creation
THE PROFESSOR
Admission 35 and 50 cents;   Reserved seats, 75 cents.[1]

Early in his career Gillette learned the importance of tryouts and advance publicity. Before it came to his home town, "The Professor" had been produced in Columbus, Ohio, during the previous summer, and in New Haven on the eve of its Hartford performance. Both Columbus and New Haven received it well, and, as might have been expected, so did Hartford. The *Courant* reviewer wrote that the acting company was well selected and superior to many such groups. Mr. Gillette, he said, was heartily received in his interpretation of the droll character of the Professor, and was accorded two curtain calls. Gillette's "Professor" was seen as a novel personality, a rather naive scientist required to marry on short notice, and proceeding about the business in the same way that he would use to solve a problem in mathematics. The plot contained many extremely ludicrous situations. In the end, the Professor redeemed himself by genuinely falling in love and revealing a sincere and appealing character. The play created an atmosphere of brightness, and was filled with witty dialogue and humorous developments. The character of the Professor, the reviewer thought, was one which like that of Lord Dundreary, could be

17

Courtesy of The Stowe-Day Foundation

Helen (Nickles) Gillette

First Successes and Marriage

developed by the playwright and actor in any number of ways. Gillette was seen to have struck "a capital vein", and could be justifiably proud of his debut as a playwright in Hartford.[2]

The *Courant* offered but one critical suggestion, namely, that a somewhat faster pace, making for more movement, would be desirable. Hartford's *Evening Post* writer, on the other hand, was frankly but gently critical, introducing his review as follows: ". . . The piece is evidently so purely amateur, both in its conception and production, that the pen of criticism is partially disarmed, and the first effort of the author must be kindly dealt with."[3]

This performance of Will Gillette's first play was a significant date in Hartford's theatrical history. On New Year's Day, Will had written from New York to the Reverend Joseph Twichell a letter, slightly brash in tone, telling him of the coming production and urging that the minister make no other commitments for January 9 and that he be allowed to save a box for him.[4] Mr. Twichell responded exactly as Will had hoped he might, with what hesitation and misgiving can only be imagined. He and his wife attended along with a large crowd of Hartford people who were not regular theatregoers; he later wrote in his journal that he could not unreservedly approve the spectacle of one of his boys on the stage, or the quality of the play.[5] Yet he and the other folk had witnessed a play, and historic ground had been broken.

About a week and a half later, "The Professor" was put on in Philadelphia. Will's sister, Lilly Warner, who was visiting in Philadelphia, saw it and wrote to her husband, George, that everything about the play had gone much more smoothly there than it had in Hartford.[6] In Philadelphia, however, Gillette met his first cold criticism. Of three critical reviews, this is typical: "The play in fact is simply a mass of rubbish, out of which now and then, is evolved something that has genuine value. Its fundamental fault is that there is no real story to tell . . . [it] seems strung together by the thinnest sort of a thread." Constructive comments were: "Mr. Gillette's representation of the professor was an example of what a clever actor can do under discouraging circumstances . . .; [it is] the work of a very young and very inexperienced playwright and actor."[7]

More than a year was to pass before "The Professor" appeared in New

York, as it eventually did with the financial help of Mark Twain.[8] Gillette turned some of his time and attention to a new venture, adapting Frances Hodgson Burnett's "Esmeralda" for the stage. The Mallory brothers, one of them an Episcopalian clergyman, who were then managing New York's Madison Square Theatre, became interested in "Esmeralda" and made of it a great hit with the cast of Annie Russell, Leslie Allen, Thomas Whiffen, and Eben Plympton. It opened in New York on October 29, 1881, and ran until the summer of 1882. Hartford had a performance in January 1884.

Percy MacKaye, in his book on his father, Steel MacKaye, tells of a letter he received from Gillette which gives a sidelight on the successful Mallorys. Will wrote: "At the Madison Square Theatre, as soon as Hazel Kirke finished its run there in June, 1881, I was stage director—but only for my own plays. Your father, though, had left awhile before that. I suppose you know that your dad had an acute row with the Mallorys—of which (which, of course you don't know) I was the storm centre, hanging on like grim death to get my play produced. My own riot with them came later. I thought better to put it off until I'd got what I wanted."[9]

When his play, "The Professor", finally opened at New York's Madison Square Theatre on June 1, Gillette fell afoul of a sober and critical reviewer who reported that it had "attracted a large and fine assemblage", and then went on to say that the play was purportedly a character study of the person called The Professor. According to the reviewer, it was, considered as a character study, weak and valueless. He labelled the play "feebly pretentious, unreal, and self-contradictory", showing no understanding of real men and women, and no skill in portraying a believable episode in true-to-life surroundings. He could not accept The Professor as a real character. The review proceeded to condemn the play for what it called a fault of many American dramatic compositions, i.e., the combination of incompatible elements, those of farce and romance. Mr. Gillette was charged with the besetting sin of a "broad and fantastic attempt to be humorous" and at the same time, a desire to contrast his humor with romance, thus making "an incongruous and coarse mixture". No freshness nor point was seen in the farce, and the romance was commonplace. The play had "neither character nor intrinsic merit, nor dramatic and social purpose". The reviewer allowed that it had some moments of mild amusement, some occasionally bright dialogue, and some good farcical effects in the last act. He allowed, too, that the setting had been charming and that the acting was on the whole intelligent. Mr. Gillette he could not credit with having made much of his part, but this might be because of his inexperience as actor and as playwright. He gave a complimentary notice to Miss Georgia Cayvan and Miss Nellie Morant.[10]

Criticism or no, "The Professor" was popular with audiences. It had a successful long run in New York, followed by a Boston engagement starting at the Park Theatre on March 20, 1882, with William Gillette and Belle Jackson in the leading roles. The *Boston Transcript* critic was generally favorable in his comments: " 'The Professor' was brought out last night before a crowded, closely interested, and as events proved, a highly entertained audience. Mr. Gillette wisely refrains from classifying his play. If it belongs distinctively to one family, it is that of farce . . . It is a mirth-provoking work, the fun consisting more in humorous dialogue and absurd *contretemps* than in wit or delicately contrived surprises . . . With one or two exceptions, there is no really fine acting, nor indeed is there much opportunity for it . . . No one of the company plays otherwise than with care and spirit, and . . . the piece goes off with a truly admirable dash. It is beautifully mounted . . . ."[11]

Gillette was making money; he was almost twenty-nine. On June 1 of 1882, he married Helen, daughter of David and Pamela Nickles (Nichols) of Detroit, Michigan. Presumably he had met her during the Cincinnati and Louisville seasons. The wedding took place in Windsor, Ontario. Guthrie Burton, second wife of Richard, Will's friend, wrote years later that in the summer of 1882, when Richard was a college student, he went with Will and his young wife, Helen, on a walking trip through the hill country of New England.[12] This may have been in Vermont from which Will had enthusiastically written his brother-in-law, George, two years earlier, calling it the prettiest place in the world, and saying he was going to build a house on one of the hills.

Marriage for Helen Gillette would mean travelling with her actor husband. The *Hartford Courant* in its announcement of the marriage spoke of Will as "known all over the country by his play 'The Professor' ". Helen liked to read, and there were relatives and friends to visit in the East, in

Courtesy of The Stowe-Day Foundation

Will Gillette as Shylock, 1875

Pennsylvania, and around Detroit. During 1883 and 1884, Will toured in "The Young Mrs. Winthrop", which a Hartford review called "one of the best and one of the pleasantest of the Madison Square comedies".[13]

On May 28, 1883, Gillette and his original Madison Square Theatre Company came to Roberts Opera House in Hartford for a farewell performance of "The Professor". The *Courant's* next day review was headed "Charming Rendition of 'The Professor' ", and went on: "Mr. Gillette was the same as ever, the inimitable, *sui generis* . . . The performance was highly satisfactory in every respect, and there are many that will regret that this very popular and meritorious play has been seen for the last time in the native city of its author."[14]

For his second success, Will drew ideas from a German play by Von Moser titled "Der Bibliothekar". The Gillette adaptation, with the title "Digby's Secretary", was presented at the New York Comedy Theatre on September 29, 1884. The review seemed to have come from the same *Times* critic who had witnessed "The Professor". He wrote that Mr. Gillette appeared quite confident of the worth of his work, and that this extended to his appearance in the title role. Quarrelling with Gillette's designation of the play as "a farcical comedy", he stated that it was plainly and simply a farce, and "rather a coarse one", with many boisterous carryings-on. His most cutting criticism was that even Gillette's work of adapting and interpreting had not been effective in ruining the original story, which was the thing of value. The cast included Frank Tannehill, T. M. Hunter, Maurice Pike, H. B. Phillips, Gertrude Johnson, Eula Talbot, Mrs. Mary Stuart, and Mme. Ivan C. Michels. Again he gave Gillette's acting faint praise, pointing out that its principal effects seemed to be attained through "extravagant" costume and a nasal manner of speaking. For other members of the cast he had commendation and praise. There were, he said, several *double entendres* that might well be left out. Then— the telling line so far as Gillette's success was concerned—he stated that the audience had been large and received the play with much laughter.[15]

On the night that "Digby's Secretary" played the Comedy Theatre, A. M. Palmer produced at the Madison Square Theatre "The Private Secretary", which had been adapted from the same German play by an Englishman named Hawtrey. Both plays were successes. A pending lawsuit between the owner of the two adaptations was settled by compromise and a combination of the best parts of each. "The Private Secretary" had a starring tour of three years and gave William Gillette a nation-wide introduction.[16]

The tour started probably in November. Will wrote his mother from St. Louis on the thirteenth that business was very good and the play going tremendously; he was to play Indianapolis, then Cincinnati. The schedule called for playing Chicago and Cincinnati on Sundays, something which he found he could not control; the arrangement troubled him, for his constitution, he said, rather than for his conscience.[17]

The Gillettes were back East for a performance in Hartford at the Opera House on December 11. Page 1 of the *Courant* announced the "Screaming Farce Comedy" with "Reserved Seats, 75¢ and $1.00", and "Admission 50¢, Gallery 25¢". The *Hartford Times* of December 12 hailed "the crack farce-comedy of the season" . . . "presented to an overflowing house by one of the Madison Square companies", . . . "so full of humor, vivacity, motion, and irresistibly comic situations that one [was] fairly delivered over into the hands of the actors"; the review ended: "Altogether the company played with great smoothness and finish, and the audience enjoyed the evening very heartily."[18]

Hartford saw "The Private Secretary" again in March 1886 at the Opera House. The review included the story of the play:

> A rich East Indian, Mr. Cattermole, returns to England to meet his nephew, Douglas, whom he has never seen, and who will be his heir when the wild-oats period of manhood is passed. Douglas is in debt to a lot of tradesmen. In order to avoid the service of a writ at the instance of Gibson, a tailor, he personates the Rev. Robert Spaulding, newly engaged as private secretary to Squire Marsland, and runs down to the latter's country-seat with a friend. Here he gets in and out of numberless scrapes. Cattermole comes to the house; so does Gibson; so does the real private secretary. Douglas conceals his identity from his uncle, satisfies his tailor's urgent demands for payment by introducing him to the squire and his family as a friend, and palms the secretary off as a spiritualistic medium on a spinster who is a believer in the materializing seance. The old East Indian has mistaken the canting old Spaulding for his nephew and this

First Successes and Marriage 25

leads to several hilarious results. Finally, the young man finds a way out of his difficulties and a wife in Edith Marsland. His uncle is glad to exchange him for the idiotic secretary, and everything comes to a jolly ending.

According to the report, the play was given one of the finished productions characteristic of the Madison Square Company. Mr. Gillette in the title role was adjudged one of the funniest characters ever seen, eliciting continual laughter; his support was excellent.[19] Receipts for this performance were $808.25, a high figure in the Opera House records.[20]

An act from "The Private Secretary", with Harry G. Richmond, William Gillette and Company, was on the program of an Elks' Benefit put on at the Boston Theatre, February 17, 1885. Other acts were McCaull Opera Company in an act from "The Sorcerer", Annie A. Park, cornetist, Henry Irving and Company in an act from "Louis XI", La Petite Louise Marguerite, the Boston Museum Company in an act from "Fantine", Margaret Mather and Frederick Paulding in a scene from "Romeo and Juliet", the Olympia Quartette, Beaudry and Lee, Manchester and Jennings, Andy and Annie Hughes, Kitty O'Neil, Harry Bloodgood, and the Imperial Banjo Quartette.[21]

In midsummer of 1885, Will and Helen were in San Francisco where both "The Professor" and "The Private Secretary" were being given. Helen wrote to her sister-in-law, Lilly, of shopping in San Francisco markets, housekeeping in two cozy little rooms, Will's happy face over breakfast coffee, visiting in Chinatown, which must be done with a policeman, and of having a China*man* for a maid. On the subject of the theatre, she reported that "The Private Secretary" had gone only fairly, with heavy expenses and competition. One week had paid expenses, but the present one with "The Professor" was not very promising. Also, Augustin Daly had just opened in San Francisco, and he was a great favorite.[22]

Will was at work on a new play—something this time quite different from "The Professor" and "The Private Secretary". "Held by the Enemy" was a five-act melodrama which became the forerunner of a long succession of Civil War dramas in the American theatre. "Held" was first produced at Brooklyn's Criterion Theatre on February 22, 1886, with Gillette as Thomas Henry Blane, war correspondent of *Leslie's Weekly,* supported by Carrie Turner and Robert Hilliard. After extensive revision, it was presented to New York on August 16, 1886, at the Madison Square Theatre with Charles S. Dickson as Blane; among the supporting players were Charles W. Stokes, Harry Woodson, and Louise Dillon.

The reviewer this time was inclined to be critical, but with fairness. He wrote that since many in the audience were actors, usually the least discriminating among theatre patrons, the play was given a demonstrative reception. Mr. Gillette's latest work, however, commanded serious consideration from beginning to end. It could not be called a profound human drama, its pathos was rather shallow, and its humor somewhat trivial. Its literary worth was not great, but its dialogue was concise and forceful, and few trite expressions were used. In sum, it was not either very great nor very powerful, but it had worth. Its setting was war, but its theme was the human heart, and the military background was of minor interest.

The story, he went on, was of the love of two soldiers for the same woman. One, a Confederate officer, had been betrothed to her since childhood; the other was a Union Colonel. The Union man was compelled to arrest the Confederate as a spy, and later had to give the evidence in a court martial which convicted the Confederate, who, had that evidence not been given, would have been held as a prisoner of war and saved from death. The woman denounced the Colonel before the court, telling of his declaration of love for her and so ascribing to him a motive for wishing the death of the Confederate. The Confederate refused to see a fellow soldier burdened by such an accusation; he said that he was a spy and proud of it. Thus the Union Colonel's character was saved, and his rival condemned to hanging. The Colonel did everything honorable to save him, but all failed, and he would not use dishonorable means. When the girl came to him and promised to be his wife if he would help her Southern lover to escape, he spurned her. The girl planned an escape and nearly succeeded. The spy was in a hospital with a severe wound, and at her suggestion, he put on an appearance of death. She obtained a permit signed by the commanding Major General, to carry a body through the lines. The Brigade Surgeon interfered and, although he respected the General's order, he thought it wise to conduct an examination. This the Colonel

Courtesy of The Stowe-Day Foundation Scene from "Held by the Enemy"

forbade; though he did not know the situation, he knew that the woman he loved had a right to custody of the body of the man whom he thought she loved. He protected her right, and ordered the Surgeon's arrest. Here the Major General intervened when the Surgeon charged the Colonel was engaging in conspiracy. To settle the dispute, the General ordered the body examined, but the spy had died, having expired during the controversy. The Colonel learned later that he himself was the man the woman loved, and the curtain fell on a promise of matrimony. The play was reported to be handsomely set, and its performance creditable.[23]

Following its New York run, "Held by the Enemy" opened on December 27, 1886 at the Boston Museum where it had a very successful season lasting until March 5, 1887. Several members of the Boston Museum Stock Company joined the cast, among them Alfred Hudson, Frank Burbeck, George W. Wilson, Kate Ryan, and May Davenport. The *Boston Transcript* critic predicted a long run for a play he chose somewhat to disapprove:

> "Held by the Enemy" is true to its name. It is an American drama, and for that reason is deserving of more attention than its intrinsic merits warrant, for it is not a great play, and it furnishes few opportunities for superior acting . . . Generally speaking, the action of the piece is rapid, and the detached scenes very effective, while the dialogue, without being remarkable at any time, is nevertheless always interesting. . . "Held by the Enemy" will be repeated until further notice—that is, it will have a long run.[24]

After the Boston performance, "Held" was taken to England and produced at the Princess Theatre in London in May 1887, and received favorable notice.[25]

Gillette's Civil War play next went out on tour under the aegis of Charles Frohman, and Will wrote his mother from San Francisco on July 16, 1887 that he and Helen were leaving the city by steamer for Santa Barbara, where they would spend three days, returning to San Francisco the following week. The company was to play a return week at the California Theatre in San Francisco, July 25–30, then start East, first to Sacramento, then Salt Lake City, Leadville, and Denver, Colorado, from

First Successes and Marriage 29

Courtesy of The Stowe-Day Foundation

Scene from "The Private Secretary"

which he would go directly to New York, and Helen would probably stop at Windsor, Ontario, for a visit.[22]

As before, Will wrote on something new while he was touring or acting in the current play. During the tour of "Held by the Enemy", he worked on "She", a play which Charles Frohman and Al Hayman had persuaded him to dramatize from Rider Haggard's romantic adventure story of the same name. Helen wrote to a relative on November 27 from New York that Will was rehearsing "She" night and day, hardly taking time to eat, and that she could not understand how he stood the strain with his nervous temperament. She said further that after the opening of "She", he was to go on the road for a seven-week season with a piece called "The Great Pink Pearl", an English comedy.[26] "She" was produced with considerable success at Niblo's Garden in New York, opening on November 29.[27] The

New York Daily Tribune reported a "long, diffuse, turbulent, pictorial, prosy spectacle" which "wearied the judicious part of a numerous audience and pleased the admirers of glare and tinsel".[28]

Will had also a play of his own to bring on called "A Legal Wreck", which opened at the Madison Square Theatre on August 14, 1888. A more tolerant reviewer, or the old one mellowed, told readers of the *New York Times* that Mr. Gillette's new play was "an odd and eccentric thing", but said that it should not be dismissed for that reason, since novelty in the theatre was to be welcomed. He found that the chief trouble with "A Legal Wreck" was that Mr. Gillette's point of view was not always clear; his audience was left uncertain when he wanted them to laugh and when he was being serious. The play was successful with the audience, more because of the personal popularity and humorous acting of Mr. Sidney Drew as the narrator than because of any of Mr. Gillette's wit, humor, and sentiment. With the removal, however, of a few defects in the somewhat bizarre play, it might be improved enough to make its points clear to everyone. The reviewer predicted that the faults would be corrected at once, since Mr. Gillette always made good use of experience.

For "A Legal Wreck", Gillette had conceived a hero betrothed to one woman and asking her to release him in order that he might marry another. The reviewer conceded that such a character was quite human, but that the playwright expected the unusual in hoping for an audience in sympathy with such a man. The whole play seemed to flout the conventional practices of the dramatic world. One strong scene involved an encounter on a cliff between a ruffian and a gentleman in love with the same girl. In the struggle the ruffian fell a considerable height onto the rocks below, and the gentleman thought himself guilty of murder. The girl who was the subject of their quarrel entered and was overwhelmed with sorrow. The narrator of the piece was on stage, as he frequently was throughout the play, and he told the gentleman that he must have killed the scoundrel and that he ought to give himself up to the law. The gentleman agreed, and the girl went home. Then the narrator lowered a rope and pulled up the rascal, not even injured, and persuaded *him* that *he* had killed the gentleman. This development was so unforeseen that the audience was non-

First Successes and Marriage

plussed. In the next act, Gillette even used the supposed murder of the rascal a second time to evoke sympathy.

The action of "A Legal Wreck" took place on the Massachusetts coast. One scene was an old sea captain's parlor with walls and ceiling of blue to suggest the ocean bottom. The Captain was an odd fellow, who kept in his sea chest an old copy of the *Calcutta Gazette,* full of shipping news of twenty years back, which he read when he was dejected. A retired second mate was his close companion. The reviewer found it a defect that the two ancient mariners spoke Oxford English rather than New England sea talk. The Captain had an adopted daughter. A young man from Boston met and fell in love with her, but the Captain's rough, drunkard son loved her, too, and raised difficulties. Soon, the narrator put in an appearance and established the girl's parentage; his aim appeared to be to set all the characters against one another for his own ends. He seemed thoroughly selfish and human. This role proved to be a "fat part" for Mr. Sidney Drew, his skillful, droll treatment of it serving to increase greatly his favor with managers and audiences. Mr. Gillette, as often, made telling use of noise to produce a realistic impression of wind and rain at the beginning and to simulate the stopping of a carriage in front of the Captain's house.[29]

The cast of "A Legal Wreck" included, besides Sidney Drew, Nina Boucicault, Boyd Putnam, George Fawcett, Alfred Hudson, Sidney Smith, Ida Vernon, Frances Graham, and Elsie Lombard.

How many of the desired changes Gillette was able to make is problematical. Helen Gillette was seriously ill. She and Will started for Hartford, but were forced to leave the train at Cos Cob, Connecticut. It was there that Helen, only twenty-eight, died on September 1, 1888 of a ruptured appendix.[30]

CHAPTER IV

Troubled years

The sudden loss of Helen was a severe shock. William Gillette could not feel himself in command; grief and loneliness wore him down to the point of protracted illness and virtual inactivity for nearly five years. The nature of Gillette's illness at this time, and in later years, is evident in letters which he wrote to Frank Fuller, one of Mark Twain's friends. Since Fuller ran a health food store and advised him on diet, etc., Will chose always to address him as "Dr.". Gillette seems to have had a tendency to digestive and intestinal disorder which was aggravated by stress and overwork.[1] This tendency may have been inherited, for he had written his brother Ed in 1883 that their mother was seriously ill with "the old enemy dysentery".[2]

Nevertheless, performances of "A Legal Wreck" continued, and Will stayed in New York for a while. George Warner saw him now and then and reported to Lilly, usually that Will looked poorly, or that he had been coming for dinner and had not showed up. He wanted the independence of hotel living, but in his present condition, it was too impersonal and certainly not adapted to the needs of any kind of invalid.[3] He spent much of the next five years in Hartford with Lilly and George and their family, and his mother, all of whom now lived in the second house which Senator Francis Gillette had built in Nook Farm. Upstairs there were secluded quarters where he could rest and write.

Playwriting became a useful source of revenue for him in these "off" years. March 3, 1890 saw the start of performances at the Boston Museum of "All the Comforts of Home" which Gillette had adapted from "Ein Toller Einfall" by Carl Lauf. The *Transcript* reviewer was forced to admit, much in spite of his critical opinion, that it would be a hit:

> It is, as Mantalini would put it, while laughing damnably that the critic must hold up Mr. Gillette's latest effort to reprobation, as a game distinctly unworthy the candle of the excellent acting which illuminates it ... Its furnishings, if one may be pardoned the metaphor, are largely of wood from the chestnut tree ...

> The play moved without a creak of the machinery from first to last. The spectator has never a moment's leisure to wonder what next . . . and best of all, the humor of the play has much in its crisp dialogue and thronging incidents . . .
>
> If this sort of thing is to be done at all—against which in passing we protest—it could not be better done than by the Museum company . . .
>
> It is to be—shall we say feared?—that the play will so catch the popular taste, with its bait of laughter, as to hold the stage indefinitely.[4]

For Gillette, as time passed, the spectators became the only critics worth heeding, and for them, his plays, even those which might seem trivial, had immense appeal. He knew that people liked to laugh and to be kept in suspense. To meet that demand, and at the same time following his own inclinations, he wrote farce and melodrama for the most part. A shrewd assessment of his own powers in writing, as well as in acting, prevented him from attempting anything larger.

When the new play opened in New York at Proctor's 23rd Street Theatre, the reviewer wrote: "As it has already had a comparatively long run in Boston, and as it is very good, as farce goes, and is uncommonly well acted, it is safe to assume that it will be successful here." He went on to say that Gillette's new piece was equally as good as several other current farces, but could not be said to compare very favorably with Mr. Daly's adaptations, and lacked the novelty and timeliness of some of the American farces turned out by Messrs. Harrigan and Hoyt. The plot involvements were skillful, whoever was responsible for them; a great deal of the dialogue, which certainly was Gillette's, was excellent. The New York cast included Henry Miller, M. A. Kennely, Ida Vernon, J. C. Buckstone, Lewis Baker, Maud Haslam, Ian Robertson, and a new young and "winsome actress of ingenue roles" who "had a congenial part".[5]

Henry Miller remembered years later that Charles Frohman was the producer of "All the Comforts" and chose for it an outstanding cast. Miller was highly pleased when he went to the initial reading and saw the accomplished actors with whom he was to work, many of them old friends. He found one stranger in the group, a diffident, rather sad-appearing young girl. Her expression was sensitive and wistful, and her manner was unusually appealing. He noticed that she was neatly, but rather shabbily

Courtesy of The Stowe-Day Foundation

Scene from "The Private Secretary"

dressed. She showed confidence, however, and addressed herself to her very small part with unusual resolution and understanding. He found himself thinking that the girl had greater possibilities and, with this in mind, he told Frohman he believed the young actress was worthy of a larger part. Frohman agreed, and said that it might be possible to have Gillette write in a small love scene with Miller for her, and that this would also help the play. The producer's interest grew as he watched rehearsals, and he finally went to Gillette in Hartford and conveyed some of his feeling about the actress. The result was that Gillette wrote in a love scene which turned out to be one of the most effective parts of the play. Miller remembered "All the Comforts" as giving him a good role and a long engagement, but his greatest pleasure was in the success achieved on the opening

Troubled Years 35

night by the young woman whom he had sponsored. The name of the actress was Maude Adams.[6]

During the fall and early winter of 1890, Will was in the Saluda Mountains of the Carolinas, at Tryon, North Carolina, which became a favored retreat. The first months of 1891 he spent in Florida and at Thomasville, Georgia; in April he wrote "Dr." Fuller from Tryon that in Florida he had lost all the weight he had gained in the Carolina mountains, and that Winter Park did not appeal to him, but he liked the Gulf Coast. A month later he wrote the "Dr." that he wanted to visit Helen's people in Windsor, Ontario. He made this trip, and not long afterward wrote from a sanatorium in Danville, New York, which he said he had been avoiding for two years.[1] It proved to be a horrible place, and he left as soon as possible for Hartford. There his friend, Dick Burton, and his wife, had been staying with the George Warners, using Will's room until he returned. When he arrived, the Burtons went to stay with the Hookers. Will was well enough in the fall to help entertain at a party given by his Aunt Isabella Hooker. The Hookers—John and Isabella—wrote their daughter early in 1892 that they had seen Will's play, "Mr. Wilkinson's Widows", which was hilarious, and added that Will was getting rich from his plays, though he was still unable to act in them.[7]

Gillette was among the first American professional dramatists to profit from the International Copyright Act of 1891 which forced American producers to start using the work of American playwrights rather than the hitherto royalty-free work of foreign writers.

"Mr. Wilkinson's Widows" opened at Proctor's Theatre in New York on March 30, 1891, and the *New York Times* reported that the new farce provoked a large audience to almost uninterrupted laughter. The odd ending of the play would, it was said, be without doubt the source of much discussion, which was probably what Gillette had intended. The piece came to an end with its central mystery unexplained, and more than that, impossible to explain rationally. Probably, however, this was the key to the whole play which the reviewer described as "a string of glittering improbabilities". In the course of the performance, such were the skill of the staging and acting, nothing seemed any more improbable than the usual ingredients of farce. The audience was in constant expectation of having the mystery cleared up in some conventional fashion, but when the curtain came down on a physically impossible situation, it somehow seemed a proper ending to a very humorous piece. There was a hint of the Gallic about it, rather naturally, since it was based on Alexander Bisson's "Feu Toupinal". The acting was said to be excellent; Mr. Joseph Holland was particularly mentioned, and others in the cast were Thomas Burns, Frederick Bond, Louise Thorndyke-Boucicault, Henrietta Crossman, and Maud White.[8]

Will went down to Tryon in the early spring of 1892, and wrote "Dr." Fuller that he was having a good bed-guest room finished in sweet pine, and further, that he would go to New York next winter and his insides could "go to hell". He had built a two-room cabin a mile from the village of Tryon where he was keeping house, making daily trips to Tryon for mail and supplies and writing amusing letters home from his estate which he had named "Thousand Pines".[3] He was an accepted part of the Tryon scene, and a welcome visitor in the mountain folks' homes near his cabin. Later, in July and August 1892, he tried an ocean trip, spending some time in France, but did not derive from it the hoped-for benefits.

Back in Hartford, he called one day on his Aunt Isabella, wife of John Hooker, and talked at some length about his theatrical plans, particularly for a new play on which he was laying out a good deal of money. She asked if his recent writing of plays and the collecting of royalties from them was not a good, safe way of making money; he agreed that it was, but said a successful production would net him a large sum, perhaps $40,000, immediately, whereas the royalty road to wealth was much slower. From his easy way of speaking, Isabella felt that Will's spirits were indeed "coming up from the grave".[7]

And so they were—so much so that the failure of "Ninety Days", which opened at the Broadway Theatre on February 6, 1893, disastrous though it was, did not daunt him. The New York critic spoke reasonably well of it:

> If anybody who sees "Ninety Days" . . . should say that it resembles another spectacular drama which has to do with Eighty Days, probably Mr. Gillette, the builder of the former, would not gainsay it. There is such a resemblance, but Mr. Gillette has got a plot [18 million dollars is

Courtesy of The Stowe-Day Foundation

Attic room, Forest Street house

Courtesy of The Stowe-Day Foundation
Will Gillette in attic room, with steam engine he constructed as a boy

left to a spinster with the proviso that she marry the son of an old friend of the testator within 90 days] and he does not take his people around the world—only from New York to Burmah, and thence to Newport . . .
 The scenery is very good and the costuming brilliant and effective . . . It is a capital thing of its kind.[9]

But the undertaking was too huge, and the public just did not care for it enough to keep coming. There were more than fifty people in the cast with hardly one well-known name among them. "Ninety Days" was a complete failure, ran barely a month, and took all of Gillette's savings. He later corrected a biographer who had put the time of his serious illness as following the failure. He did retire to Tryon and wrote "Dr." Fuller about a leaking roof. He said he was far from "a lemon" [his play, presumably] which nevertheless remained sour and was nothing he wanted; he was thinking of lecturing, he wrote.[10] Instead he busied himself with a new play, but first took a Thousand Islands cruise and spent some time in his beloved Vermont.

At no time in his life did Will lack the comfort and consolation of feminine society. Helen had gone—her lovely, bright presence—but there were still his mother, his sister Lilly, fifteen years his senior, and among others, two charming youngsters, the Beecher girls, Mary Frances and Margaret, twins who had been adopted by James and Frances (Johnson) Beecher. They lived now at Cos Cob, Connecticut, and were always glad to walk with him and bring or leave him tokens of flowers. Of the two it was May (Mary Frances) who became closer. Will and May's correspondence, begun in 1889, seems to have lapsed until 1894, but was then resumed. By then, the twins were seeing college students, and Margie married in 1895. Will, forty-two, seems not clearly to have judged the effect he had on May. *He* had made a promise to Helen never to marry again; he kept the promise. For him the pleasure of May's attention and feeling for him was enough. May, and May's mother, saw things otherwise, for May was in love enough to want to marry. Her mother wrote Will that May could overlook his age and religious views, and urged him, for May's and his own sake, to forget his promise not to remarry. This Will could not do. May and Will saw less of each other and their correspondence waned. May eventually married, but kept Will's letters in her possession. They remained

Troubled Years

on good terms and Will wrote now and then offering to get tickets for plays.[11]

There was another close feminine influence in Will's life—that of Sophie, wife of Edward, Gillette's older brother. Ed was thirteen, Sophie only eight years older than Will. Will seems to have had a romantic feeling toward his sister-in-law, and made her his confidante in the first homesick letters written in 1873 from St. Louis and New Orleans. He later became her loyal and loving support in the time of her conflict with and ultimate divorce from Ed. At least one element in the conflict appears to have been the differing views of Sophie and Ed about Chester Turney, an ex-convict.[2] Will's affection and concern for Sophie's situation may well have helped to bring him out of *his* "grave".

So much were Will's spirits rising that even his mother's death at the end of 1893, on December 16, did not cause a real relapse. He had been very close to his mother; he felt protective toward her, they were kindred in mind and spirit; with her gone he felt and said that Hartford was no longer his real home. But he was now on the mend, with a new play up his sleeve and more important, the will and energy for acting in it.

CHAPTER V

Acting again in his own plays

Something had given Gillette the will to look out again and live. He might have remained for the rest of his life the half-invalid recluse he had been since Helen's death. Gertrude Lynch wrote that "Nobody expected William Gillette to come back to civilization alive from his hut in North Carolina".[1] He himself wrote to "Dr." Fuller in 1906 that he remembered what had caused his recovery ("upward start", he called it) about three years after he had first visited Fuller's health food store in the early 90's, as an emaciated wreck. He then asked the doctor whether he had ever told him the reason and added that he thought he had told no one.[2] What was it?—in part, perhaps, the adoring love of May Beecher, perhaps the friendship of the North Carolina mountain folk, one of whom, tradition said, had nursed him back to health after his collapse on a mountain path; or it may have been his feeling for and concern over Sophie. Possibly it was all of these, and the North Carolina mountain retreat itself where he could build a place of his own in his own way among friends who asked no questions. A visitor to Tryon brought back for the *Boston Herald* a story of Gillette's retreat, including the statement: "Everyone in Tryon knows him and loves him, not as Gillette, the famous actor and playwright . . . but Gillette the man, the kind, good-natured, funny gentleman, who always has the right thing to say to the children and gives you a word, too, that makes the day seem brighter just for his passing."[3] Some of the May Beecher story and some of his North Carolina experience went into a later play titled "Clarice".

Meantime, a friendship was developing which came to mean much to him, both professionally and personally. A young entrepreneur in the theatre world, by name Charles Frohman, had booked Gillette's early plays, "The Professor" and "The Private Secretary", at the Madison Square Theatre. Frohman and his partner, Al Hayman, had together persuaded Gillette to do the dramatization of "She". Frohman had booked "Held by the Enemy" on the road, then when the tour ended, took the

40

play and the company, including Gillette, for an engagement at the Baldwin Theater in San Francisco.

Frohman brought into Gillette's theatre life a buoyant good humor and optimism which the latter often needed in difficult times. In San Francisco, for instance, the critics were hard on "Held by the Enemy". Gillette was feeling downcast as he read the papers, when along came Frohman "in his usual cheery fashion. 'Look what the critics have done to us,' said Gillette gloomily. 'But we've got all the best of it,' replied Frohman with animation. 'How's that?' asked Gillette, somewhat puzzled. *'They've* got to stay here!' "[4]

Gillette's play was in fact the source of much profit for Charles Frohman and among the first of a succession of plays on Civil War themes. Bronson Howard's "Shenandoah", probably the most successful, was a financial and professional goldmine for Frohman.[5]

"C.F.", as Frohman was called by his friends, was "an incoherent and shy little man whose inability to express himself amounted almost to a vocal impediment. But perhaps through some sort of telepathy and an actor's intuitive receptiveness, he was always able to make himself understood."[6] He had an instinctive sensitivity for what was good, theatrically and humanly speaking. William Gillette was one of those whom Frohman chose not only as a star and a potentially successful theatre person, but as a personal friend.

Early in 1894, Gillette attended a performance of "A Doll's House", only its second in English on the New York stage since Ibsen had written it twenty years before. Mrs. Minnie Maddern Fiske starred, and Gillette "scooped all the critics with the first written acclaim. After Mrs. Fiske had received Ibsen's wreath and taken her last curtain call, Gillette . . . borrowed writing materials at the theatre office, and sent her a message: BY JOVE! The two words, printed large on a sheet of notepaper, had a look of stunned surprise."[7] Gillette was always generous with praise and encouragement for his colleagues, particularly the actresses.

His own next play was being prepared and, this time, he had again adapted a French farce, "La Plantation Thomassin", and gave it the English title, "Too Much Johnson". Will took the leading role as Augustus Billings, his first acting since the death of his wife. Frohman was the producer, and there were tryouts at Waltham and Springfield, Massachusetts. At Waltham, "the house was small and the notices bad. Frohman joined the company next day at Springfield. Gillette was much depressed, and he met Frohman in this mood. 'This is terrible, isn't it? I'm afraid the play is a failure.' 'Nonsense!' said Frohman. 'I have booked it for New York and for a long tour afterward.' 'Why?' asked Gillette in astonishment. 'I saw your performance,' was the reply."[8]

"Too Much Johnson" played briefly in Brooklyn and then opened at the Standard Theatre in New York on November 26, 1894. The reviewer noted that there was a good house which gave Gillette's adaptation from the French the warm reception which it deserved. Gillette himself, he said, had given a lively interpretation of the role of the inventor of "the mythical Johnson", and the merits of the play were sufficient to make it well worth a visit. In the critic's view, Mr. Gillette's productions as playwright and actor were always well executed and his technique excellent. The company had come from Brooklyn unchanged and was quite capable.[9]

What this reviewer chose to call "the little play" was thought interesting enough to be revived in an adaptation seventy years later, in 1964, and presented for two weeks off Broadway. Edith Oliver in the *New Yorker* gave a good idea of how a farce of the 1890's, a Gillette farce, struck a theatregoer of the 1960's:

> I had an awfully good time at the revival of William Gillette's "Too Much Johnson" . . . The plot . . . doesn't exactly defy, but certainly resists an analysis. It is compounded of mistaken identity, cross-purposes, interrupted mail, opening and closing doors, any amount of hokum, and all the other priceless and ageless elements of farce. The time is 1896; the settings are a cruise ship bound for Cuba and a plantation on the island, and the Johnson of whom there is too much is really *two* Johnsons —a fake one and a real one.[10]

Howard Taubman in the *New York Times* wrote of the 1964 production that there were moments when its "sheer balminess" was delightful, and others when the farce seemed "rustier and creakier than a buggy that [hadn't] been used in seven decades".[11] Walter Kerr in the *Herald Tribune* said he didn't know that the piece would be unusually funny however done in 1964, but that there might be "a temperate, mildly clever way of doing it that would also do justice to its glib and rather sunny manner . . . at least once in the evening [he] saw a gesture that seemed effortlessly in charge of itself . . . Ah, [he] thought, I'll bet that's the way William Gillette did it. No fuss. No feathers. Finesse."[12]

While the 1894 "Too Much Johnson" was on the boards, Will was making final revisions in another Civil War melodrama. Frohman had been about to sail for Europe when Will sent him the first act of "Secret Service". Frohman asked for the second act, then postponed his trip to Europe until he had seen the whole play. Remembering the success of "Held by the Enemy" and "Shenandoah", he foresaw another hit.[13]

"Secret Service" opened in Philadelphia at the Broad Street Theatre on May 13, 1895, with Maurice Barrymore, father of Lionel, Ethel, and John, in the leading role. Walter Pritchard Eaton stated that Barrymore was a splendid and romantic actor, but he was "not keyed to the style in which Gillette was working".[14] Though the play went well in Philadelphia, Gillette decided that it needed revision, and Barrymore contributed to this.[15] The New York opening finally took place at the Garrick Theatre on October 5, 1896, with Gillette in the dual role of Lewis Dumont-Captain Thorne. Gillette succeeded in creating a spy who was the hero of the play.

The *New York Times* critic of "Secret Service" wrote that Gillette's plays were usually successful and deservedly so. The new one, he said, merited high praise, but whether it would be given a long run seemed doubtful. It was a melodrama, plainly enough, but was unusual in that it made delicate, rather than "sledge-hammer", appeals to the emotions. Gillette in his drama of love and war used dialogue and action which were both "elliptical in much the same way that [his] acting [was] often elliptical". In some of the most crucial moments, he hinted rather than set forth, thus leaving much to the imagination and intelligence of the audience. Perhaps all of his hints would not serve, and it was in this element that the play's weakness lay.

As Captain Thorne, Union spy, the reviewer said Mr. Gillette had a part made to order which he acted with his characteristic coolness and finesse. Miss Amy Busby, in the role of Edith Varney, Thorne's Southern sweetheart, was somewhat inadequate, but her efforts were commendable. Odette Tyler, in a small juvenile part, scored the hit of the evening. Among others in the cast were Campbell Gollan, Ida Waterman, and Walter Thomas.[16]

"Secret Service" had "an enormous run" at the Garrick,[17] continuing until March 6, 1897. It opened two days later at the Boston Museum and drew a large attendance until April 24. The *Boston Transcript* went all out in praise of it, saying: "At last we have a drama which commands thorough respect—in dignity of theme, in coherence of action and plot, in vitality of characters, in everything that goes toward the making of a powerful play."[18]

Sometime in late 1896 or early 1897, Charles Frohman sent John Drew, another of his stars, a telegram which read: "WOULD ETHEL LIKE TO GO TO LONDON WITH GILLETTE IN SECRET SERVICE?" Frohman had indeed booked "Secret Service" for the Adelphi Theatre in London where it opened on May 15, 1897. Ethel Barrymore had the small role of Miss Kittredge who sewed for the hospital, and Odette Tyler had the leading comedy part. One night when Miss Tyler was ill, Ethel had to step into her role, without Miss Tyler's costume which she had worn away with her, played the part, and made a hit.[19]

The *London Times* greeted Gillette with a very favorable notice for his first appearance on the London stage:

> America has sent over a good play, and *Secret Service*—whatever may be thought of it as a melodrama—without sensation, without din and smoke and gun powder, must command attention as the work of a singularly clever playwright and actor, and as the very best example we have yet seen of harmonious, easy, and well-balanced acting, seldom obtained from overseas.[20]

Even George Bernard Shaw found good things to say of Gillette in a generally critical article:

> "Secret Service" at the Adelphi, with a smart American cast, is pure regulation melodrama . . . It has a capital situation, in Mr. Gillette's best style, at the end of the second act. But this, like all the other situations, takes a huge deal of leading up to, and leads to nothing itself, being so

speedily forgotten that before half an hour has elapsed the heroine quite forgets that it has involved, apparently, an act of fratricide on the part of the hero. The hero, by the way, is a spy . . . he first spied on the South, and then, at the critical moment, betrays the North for purely personal reasons. Altogether an unredeemed rascal. But Mr. Gillette plays him with so manly an air that the audience does not stop to ask what it is applauding; and everybody seems delighted. I confess I was disappointed; for I am an admirer of Mr. Gillette's *Held by the Enemy* which seemed to me a new departure in the melodrama and an excellent play into the bargain. His *Secret Service* is not to be compared to it. Miss Odette Tyler almost bewitched us into believing that the comic relief was funny, especially in the scene with the telegraph operator . . . who acted excellently.[21]

Gertrude Stein, with Gillette's melodramas in mind, later paid tribute to his technique of "silence stillness and quick movement". She said that it had been done already by villains "particularly in such plays as The Queen of Chinatown and those that had to do with telegraph operators", but that Gillette "had conceived it and it made the whole stage the whole play this technique silence stillness and quick movement . . . In fact Gillette created what the cinema later repeated by mixing up the short story and the stage."[22]

Gillette's visit to England, the first of many, was enjoyable. England that summer was celebrating the Diamond Jubilee of Queen Victoria. But eight theatre appearances a week in strange surroundings were exhausting; he was trying at the same time to work on a new play. By early July, Gillette was ill, and reports went around that he would be forced to retire from the stage and from playwriting. He spent several days in bed under the care of physicians and nurses. The *New York Tribune* printed a story on July 10, with dateline London July 9, which stated that an understudy had taken over his part, but that the fact of his breakdown had been withheld from the public and his name had been kept on the playbills. On the advice of physicians, Gillette returned to New York. The voyage and cessation of work were beneficial. He told a *Tribune* reporter interviewing him on his return in early August that he had been ill for two weeks, but was now all right. Questioned about prejudice against American actors in London, he said the English had spoiled them by cheering at the end of every act; the play was such a success that he had gone for four weeks and ended by staying three months.[23]

"Secret Service" was indubitably a "hit" play. Gillette had recovered sufficiently by mid-August to form a new company, and "Secret Service" began another American run at Frohman's Empire Theatre in New York on September 1, 1897. The *New York Tribune* reported on September 2 that Gillette was "as icily calm and as calmly convincing and effective as before".

In England after Gillette's breakdown, a fellow member of the company had stepped into his difficult dual role. Later a new group of players formed at the Adelphi headed by the well-known actor, William Terriss. After a brief closing for vacations, performances were resumed on November 24, 1897. The run was tragically suspended on December 16, 1897 by the murder of Terriss at the stage door of the playhouse. Terriss was stabbed three times by a crazed fellowplayer, William Archer Prince, and died twenty minutes later. His funeral was attended by many theatre celebrities including John Drew, Charles Frohman, Henry Irving, and William Gillette who, following engagements in the United States, had returned to London to conclude some business matters with the Adelphi management.[24]

"Secret Service" continued its run. Hartford had it for four nights March 21–24, 1898, and Frohman took it to San Francisco in November. In 1899 it ran again in Hartford for three nights, March 16–18, and for a one-night stand December 16, the latter as a benefit for the Yacht Club. In 1900, Frohman made "Secret Service" his first Paris production at the Théâtre Renaissance, with the great French actor, Lucien Guitry, in the leading role of Captain Thorne-Lewis Dumont. The atmosphere of the play did not come through to the French, and there was the old trouble—they could not decide whether it was a serious or comic play. The character of General Nelson was almost completely omitted because the actors themselves could not decide whether it was meant to be humorous or tragic.[25]

In the midst of his Boston engagement, in early 1897, Will had taken time to write his artist friend, Amelia Watson, that next spring everything in his Tryon cabin would be in running order. Gillette had started collecting her water colors in 1896, and in July of that year asked her to make

Acting Again in His Own Plays 47

up for him a Florida book putting in the exquisite tiny scenes of which he had seen examples in her sketch books.[26]

Apart from pleasant plans and pursuits like these, there was ever more work and business in his theatre world.

CHAPTER VI

Sherlock Holmes, etc.

The late 1890's were Gillette's busiest years in the theatre. To performances of the long-run "Secret Service" and to writing, he now added commuting to England for acting and on business. It was a full life and a healthy one.

Hartford had its first view of "Secret Service" with Gillette in March 1898. There was an unprecedented sale of seats and a matinee was added to the schedule. On the opening night, Gillette received an ovation, and the curtain calls were so many that he departed from custom and made a speech at the end of the third act. The *Courant's* review included this appraisal: "William Gillette himself shows in his acting as he shows in this play a lack of display and theatrical effect which have won him much of his fame . . . he never seems to be taking the trouble to act but seems as if he were actually living the part."[1]

"Too Much Johnson" was due for an April 18 opening at the Garrick Theatre in London, and before leaving to show the English his Augustus Billings, Gillette wrote actress Annie Russell, another young favorite, asking her to address him at the Garrick.[2] This would be his second appearance on the London stage.

Gillette wrote "Dr." Fuller from London on July 9 saying that he would be leaving London in about two weeks and that when he reached New York (which he did on July 28), he would have about one week in which to visit his sister at the old house in Hartford where his better life had been lived, arrange business matters there, attend to New York business, go out for a cruise in his boat, see a few relatives, and go to Vermont to look for a place for his farm.[3] Gillette was feeling rushed. This is the first mention of a farm in Vermont and of his boat. He had two boats and by this time was probably cruising in the one called "Aunt Polly", perhaps christened after the North Carolina mountain woman who was said to have cared for him during his illness. "Aunt Polly" was described, probably facetiously and possibly by Gillette himself, as a cumbersome craft, sixty feet long and

Courtesy of The Stowe-Day Foundation   William Gillette in "Sherlock Holmes"

about as wide, propelled by a sewing machine motor, and in a fair wind able to make two and a quarter knots.[4] A Des Moines reporter who seemed to have talked with Gillette's niece, Ivey, Sophie's daughter, a frequent passenger on "Aunt Polly", came closer to the truth when he described her as an up-to-date steam launch and "a little palace afloat", artistically furnished with Turkish rugs, easy chairs, and book cases.[5] As cabin boy for the "Aunt Polly", Gillette had engaged a young Japanese, Yukitaka Osaki, who was to become his valet and dresser. The reference in Gillette's letter to Fuller to a farm in Vermont indicates that he was now looking for a place of his own in the New England area.

In August he wrote from Hartford to Amelia Watson regretting that she and her friend, Miss Morley, had decided against occupying the North Carolina cabin because they felt opening it would be too difficult. He renewed his offer, saying that his sister and brother (Lilly and George Warner) "got it going" and Miss Watson and Miss Morley should be able to do so. He spoke of his intention to build a smaller cabin, with large fireplace, for friends, and hoped that, at the least, they would use that sometime, and finally remarked that she must know it to be a good place to stay, even if she had sketched it all. He also ordered $200 worth of water color sketches from Miss Watson.[6]

November found Gillette in San Francisco for an engagement of "Secret Service". Charles Frohman, having cleared preliminaries with British author, Sir Arthur Conan Doyle, wired Gillette to begin his dramatization of the already popular Sherlock Holmes detective stories. Will engaged another actor to play his role in "Secret Service" and left the company at San Diego.[7] Within three to four weeks, the manuscript of "Sherlock Holmes" was completed with the help of W. G. Postance.[8] Sir Arthur Conan Doyle himself had written a five-act drama on Sherlock which he later turned over to Charles Frohman who then gave it to Gillette. Gillette was eager to play Sherlock and asked for "permission to rewrite according to his own discretion. The author [Sir Arthur Conan Doyle], by this time bored with the whole matter, agreed. It got itself so thoroughly re-written into another play that nobody now knows what the original play was about. Then, after a long silence, came Gillette's cable: MAY I MARRY HOLMES? The answer to this, of course, should have been a quiet and simple, 'No', backed up, if necessary with a butcher's cleaver. But [Sir Arthur] Conan Doyle merely replied that Gillette could marry Holmes or murder him or do anything he liked with him."[9]

Gillette's first draft of the "Sherlock" play was in the hands of his secretary who was staying at the Baldwin Hotel in San Francisco. The Baldwin caught fire during the night and the secretary barely escaped with his life, leaving the manuscript in the burning building. He went to tell Gillette at the Palace Hotel. Gillette queried, "Is this hotel on fire?" To the answer, "No, indeed", Gillette replied, "Well, come and tell me all about it in the morning."[10] Re-writing was apparently no problem.

Gillette had completed another play which opened at the Madison Square Theatre on January 16, 1899. "Because She Loved Him So" was another farce adapted from the French, and, "one of the most delightful features of the theatre season".[11]

From Hartford on January 22, 1899, Will wrote Annie E. Trumbull, fellow Hartford Public High School graduate and later Hartford blue stocking, sending her in New York a note of introduction to Daniel Frohman. He said he was glad to hear that she was looking with more favor on Jewish theatre people, since he considered them far better than the representatives of other races in the theatrical business. Again on January 27, he wrote her from New York saying he *knew* she would leave New York (as she had) as soon as he returned. His schedule called for acting (probably in "Secret Service") in Philadelphia, two weeks in Brooklyn beginning February 6, then a week each in Harlem, Baltimore, and Washington, with a brief engagement in Hartford after that. He made a generous offer, if she would come to any of these places (though he knew it futile to suggest), to have her met with carriages, escorted to her stopping place, then to the theatre where he would have a box for her with roses in it, and then have her taken from the theatre home or to the station; he would do the same at Hartford if she would only *arrive* from somewhere.[12] Between the two there ran a lifelong friendship in which Will seems to have played the role of teasing elder brother.

While in Hartford on January 24, he had written Amelia Watson saying enthusiastically that just *one* of the water colors she had delivered the day before would be worth the whole $200, adding that if she wished to hasten the completion of the North Carolina cabin, she should pray for the failure of "Sherlock Holmes"—he himself sometimes did just that![6]

"Secret Service" had another run in Hartford, this time for three nights, March 16–18, 1899, at Parsons Theatre. The *Courant* review referred to the spy play as "one of the most intense and powerful dramas that have appeared on our stage".[13]

In early spring of 1899, Gillette went to England for Sir Arthur Conan Doyle's approval of his "Sherlock Holmes". During the week of his fortieth birthday, in May, Sir Arthur Conan Doyle invited Gillette to his home at Undershaw for the week end to read the manuscript. Gillette arrived dramatically, play in hand and wearing the Sherlock costume he had prepared. A biographer of Sir Arthur Conan Doyle wrote: "Not even Sidney Paget had done it so well in a drawing. The clear-cut features, the deep-set eyes, looked out under a deerstalker cap; even Gillette's age, the middle forties, was right . . . ."[14]

On Gillette's return from Europe at the end of June, he reported to the press that he had been having long conferences with Sir Arthur Conan Doyle on the matter of the stage version of "Sherlock Holmes", which was to open in the autumn. He said that the work of fitting the play for the stage was his, but if it failed, he should not be repeating that in a curtain speech. Sir Arthur Conan Doyle had the manuscript for a few final touches. The season would begin out of town, and after a few weeks, Gillette would bring it to New York's Garrick Theatre.[15]

"Sherlock Holmes" had its first performance anywhere at the Star Theatre in Buffalo, New York, on October 23, 1899, and its first New York City performance at the Garrick Theatre on November 6. The New York critic had this to say:

> Sherlock Holmes's triumph on the stage will equal if not fairly surpass his triumph in the circulating libraries . . .
>
> Mr. Gillette, in his play which was received with an unmistakable demonstration of approval . . . has successfully preserved the humor of Sherlock Holmes in transferring him to the stage . . .
>
> In the manner of production there is a sort of novelty that pleases, too. The curtain is never seen to rise or fall. Each picture is slowly revealed out of darkness and fades from the view at the climax. Every device of modern stage mechanism used is used with admirable skill . . .

Courtesy of The Stowe-Day Foundation

Scene from "Clarice"

> As for the acting, Mr. Gillette looks his part and carries it in his accustomed nonchalant and pictorially effective way.[16]

The rest of the story is history—the history of an all-time theatre success piece and of a literary character who became identified with the appearance of the actor who portrayed him on the stage. Gillette played "Sherlock" more than 1300 times, in numerous revivals, and with box office receipts of over $1,500,000. In the play, too, he popularized the fade-out, or gradual darkening of the stage before the final curtain.

The essential appeal of Gillette's "Sherlock Holmes" lived through many revivals. A 1915 reviewer found that the play was "lifted by a genuine and telling characterization". He went on: "It is great fun to see once more an exhibition of such unabashed theatricalism, such unblushing working-up of an entrance, for instance. The scene is a luxurious ambush of crime. A woman's screams are heard above, and before your eyes a safe is cracked. A fair prisoner is just being tortured to make her reveal the hiding place of priceless papers when the door bell rings. A secret window affords the villainess a glimpse of the unwelcome visitor. It is a tall, thin man. 'Sherlock Holmes', murmurs the burglar, and departs by way of a window. There is a hasty assumption of calm. The rather suspect butler passes along the lighted hallway to the door. Portentous silence. Banging of door. More portentous silence, broken only by the rustle of murmurous anticipation from the other side of the footlights. And then, and then, there appears in the doorway—Sherlock Holmes."[17]

One of many, Elmer Rice's is probably the best personal report of what it was like to see Gillette's "Sherlock Holmes":

> In the climactic scene of the play the master-mind of Baker Street, pursued by the sinister Professor Moriarty, takes refuge in the Stepney Gas Chamber. Warned of the approach of the Professor, he looks about for some means of escape and then, as the door opens, he quickly puts out the lights. The stage is in complete darkness; nothing is visible except the glowing end of the cigar Holmes has been smoking. We cannot see Moriarty and his confederates enter, but we can hear them. "Follow the cigar!" shouts Moriarty. There is excited movement, then curses, followed by the switching on of the lights. Then we see that the wily Holmes has placed the cigar on the sill of one window and made his escape through another.

It may all sound rather ridiculous, but it would be impossible to exaggerate the effect it had upon the audience. Shivers and exclamations of apprehension were followed by relief that expressed itself in delighted laughter and sustained applause. I saw the play in 1911, and all I remember of the text is what I have quoted; but I shall never forget the lean and agile Gillette, in his deer-stalker's cap, or the excitement of that scene.[18]

The "conception of the character of Sherlock Holmes was entirely created by Mr. Gillette" according to the illustrator Frederick Dorr Steele, who goes on:

This is a good place to answer the question so often asked, "Which came first, Gillette's play or Steele's pictures?" The play first saw the calcium in 1899, but *The Return of Sherlock Holmes* with my pictures was not published until four years later. Everybody agreed that Mr. Gillette was the ideal Sherlock Holmes, and it was inevitable that I should copy him. So I made my models look like him, and even in two or three instances used photographs of him in my drawings. But while the actor was seen by thousands, the magazines and books were seen by millions; so after a score of years had gone by, few could remember which "did it first".[19]

Gillette's home town saw performances of "Sherlock Holmes" before Boston and before England. He brought the company to Hartford October 25–27, 1900, and the *Courant* reviewer wrote:

. . . The play is a melodrama, first, last, and all the time. Badly set and played, it would be merely a shocker . . . It is good stagecraft; the interest of the audience is not allowed to lag for an instant. And the settings and accessories are as complete as they always are in Gillette's plays.
. . . Of William Gillette's acting much has been said and so long as he chooses to act much will be said. Many proclaim him as the most finished and polished actor of the day, the acme of realism; others say he simply acts William Gillette in any part he may have to play. Perhaps the mean of these two extremes is nearest the truth. In many things very finished, in coolness and quickness; in many things very Gillette in manner and speech . . .[20]

The same paper reported that Gillette had been entertained by members of the Twilight Club the evening before at the Hartford Club. Hartford had "Sherlock" again for two nights in December, and the *Courant* critic wrote on this occasion that Mr. Gillette should be proud of such an audience on the second visit of the same play to Hartford. He continued: "Though the play thrilled and the company and settings were appreciated, what the people really flocked to see was William Gillette and him they saw in a part which he helped build and which fits his dramatic methods excellently."[21]

Boston had a five-week run of "Sherlock" at the Hollis Street Theatre from February 18 to March 23, 1901. Between the Boston and English seasons, presumably Gillette had a holiday in North Carolina. Then on September 2, 1901, "Sherlock" opened at the Shakespeare Theatre in Liverpool, England, and, in the words of John Dickson Carr, "on September 9th, in the huge Lyceum Theatre [in London] with its caverns of gilt and red plush, William Gillette appeared in what was subtitled 'A hitherto unpublished episode in the career of the great detective, and showing his connection with the STRANGE CASE OF MISS FAULKNER.' Sherlock Holmes was shown lounging at Baker Street in embroidered slippers and a flowered-silk dressing gown. Madge Larrabee (the villainess) depicted modishness in a full-tailed skirt sweeping dust from the stage, and a beige velvet hat trimmed with a large white bird. It was not exactly an unpublished episode. In Gillette's version, half a dozen reminiscences of past plots hovered through the action as Holmes recovered the compromising papers, or faced a soft-voiced Professor Moriarty dressed to resemble Mr. Pickwick. There was one disturbing incident; a part of the gallery couldn't hear the actors and said so loudly. One or two critics complained of Americanisms in the dialogue . . . But it ended in a triumph."[22]

Sir Arthur Conan Doyle wrote in his autobiography: "It was written and most wonderfully acted by William Gillette, the famous American. Since he used my characters and to some extent my plots, he naturally gave me a share in the undertaking, which proved to be very successful. . . I was charmed both with the play, the acting and the pecuniary result."[23]

On November 12, 1901, a London paper denied the report recently printed in America and cabled to London that an engagement existed between William Gillette and Maud Fealy, his attractive leading lady in

Courtesy of The Stowe-Day Foundation

Scene from "Diplomacy"

"Sherlock Holmes". Maud's mother, Margaret Fealy, was in the same company, she forty-eight, and Maud seventeen. The same news story stated that Mr. Gillette had by no means abandoned his idea of playing Hamlet, and was then planning the production which would include a new Hamlet in a more cohesive play, with plainer motives, and sumptuously mounted.[24] The idea for "Hamlet" seems to have come originally from a suggestion made by Sophie, Will's sister-in-law. He replied to her on January 27, 1898 from Philadelphia: "What an odd idea that was of yours about my playing *Hamlet*—I seem so little adapted to such a thing. Did you really mean it? You interest me."[25]

Gillette wrote "Dr." Fuller from the Savoy Hotel on December 1 saying he expected to be in England until April 1, 1902 and reported continued loss of weight.[3] Sir Arthur Conan Doyle invited all of the American members of the "Sherlock Holmes" company to Undershaw for Christmas Day, 1901, saying he could accommodate all with great ease, including Miss Fealy's mother, and holding out the prospect of seeing a little of English country life.[26]

On February 1, Gillette's play was seen by royalty. Edward VII and Queen Alexandra came to the evening performance and following the curtain, the king visited Gillette in his dressing room. On April 3, Gillette sponsored a farewell dinner for London friends in the Beefsteak Room atop the Lyceum Theatre. In attendance were the American ambassador, Joseph M. Choate, Sir Henry Irving, Ellen Terry, Arthur W. Pinero, Charles Frohman, J. Comyns Carr, Mr. and Mrs. Beerbohm Tree, H. B. Irving, Anthony Hope, Cecilia Loftus, Lawrence Irving, Charles Wyndham, John Hare, and Forbes Robertson.

"Sherlock Holmes" ended its long run in London on April 11, 1902, and Gillette set out on a road tour which went as far north as Edinburgh. From the Windsor Hotel in Glasgow, he wrote "Dr." Fuller on April 21 that he would be getting home about June 1. He arrived in Boston on the Cunarder *Ivernia* on June 19, and proceeded directly to Hartford. Less than a week later, he wrote "Dr." Fuller from Greenport, Long Island, where he was seeing about his boat which had wintered there. He told the "Dr." that he was resting, that he was not ill, but "much worn".[3]

CHAPTER VII

More acting and a new play

In the busy theatre of the 1880's, 1890's, and early 1900's, Gillette was eminently successful and achieved a position all his own. He was unique in being for many of his plays the author, leading actor, stage director, and business manager. He liked it that way. Some of his most finished acting, however, came in later years when he was actor only.

The American theatre of Gillette's time was perhaps more rich and varied than at any period since. In the national and international theatre, there were truly great actors and actresses, such as Booth, Irving, Bernhardt, Duse, Salvini, Coquelin, and Modjeska, all of them exponents of the romantic, poetic, and tragic drama. Gillette did not belong in the company of these great ones. This he knew, and apparently he had no feelings of inadequacy or of waste of his talents because he did not essay more dramatic roles. The one attempt he made in this direction was forestalled.

Otis Skinner said that Gillette had a "particularly virulent case of *Hamlet,* and it progressed to the point of a complete scenic and costume equipment of the play".[1] The story is told that when Sir Herbert Beerbohm Tree, the English actor, heard that William Gillette would act Hamlet, he snapped, "Fine actor", in his high-pitched voice, biting off each phrase. "Very fine actor. Going to play Hamlet, is he? I wonder if he'll have any new lighting effects."[2] Gillette did indeed work on a production of "Hamlet", with Frohman's approval. Frohman, however, must have been somewhat less than enthusiastic about a Shakespeare production, for when he read Barrie's "The Admirable Crichton", he told Gillette he had just the play for him, whereupon all plans for "Hamlet" were dropped, and the scenery and costumes went into storage. It is probable that the diversion from Hamlet to Crichton gave Gillette a notable success and saved him from very possible adverse criticism, since he intended to make drastic changes in "Hamlet" and its customary stage presentation.

Before starting rehearsals for the Barrie play, Will had a good rest on

```
SEVENTH SISTER                    HADLYME
                                  CONNECTICUT
                        March the 7th - 1927
```

Dear Mr. Briggs -- of Harper & Brothers:--
          I am putting an alias (if that is
a correct name for it) on the outside of the envelope
doomed to convey this letter, in order to trick you
into opening it. I am only too well aware that you
would shrink from doing so if you knew ahead that
it came from me -- fearing that I would have something
in it that would delay the manufacture of the book
you are making out of my story. So far from doing that
am I, that I (as before, verbally) now beg you in type-
writing, not to send me the Page Proof -- for of course
I know my weakness. I am very & extremely tired of the
thing now, and would want to change everything.
          Also you can realize my overwhelming desire to
have the book make the April date instead of having it
go over to May, when I tell you that I have finally
found the paragraph which was my favorite of the whole
damn thing -- and not only that, but of great value to
"centralizing" the character of Pentecost --(which he so
much needs) and which Miss Rose ruthlessly crossed out;--
yet not for a minute would I hold up the book to get it in.
          No, Mr. Briggs -- that story of mine has handicaps
enough without the crowning one of making it a May publication. So you must believe me when I state, that this
letter is to thank you for "The Ways of Life"— which has
just come from you by mail, and for "Tomorrow Morning"
which I took with me as spoils from your office when
last there, and which I am enjoying to my utmost limit.
Surely that Anne Parrish creature beats the very dogs--
to say nothing of the very cats. She is certainly at
the top of the list, and I am exultant that we have
her here in the U. S. A.
                    As ever   *William Gillette*

✕✕
I throw in that cut out paragraph referred
to above, so that you can see I am not
talking about nothing -- although I do
not expect you to comprehend why I should
feel that it has any particular value.

Courtesy of The Connecticut Historical Society

A Gillette letter

More Acting and a New Play

"Aunt Polly". On September 30 he wrote Lilly from Newport Harbor that he was stormbound, but relishing the northeasters, open fires, exercise, working on his part, reading, and generally enjoying himself. He had been held for three days at Provincetown and arrived at Cottage City, Martha's Vineyard, just after Amelia Watson had left—unfortunate, for he had wanted to see her. In a postscript he referred to Gustav Kobbé's article on him in the *Ladies Home Journal,* saying it contained so much "ridiculous stuff" and that the only thing right in it was his birth date [which was the erroneous one of 1855!].[3]

The Barrie play opened at the Lyceum Theatre on November 17, 1903, with Gillette in the role of the butler Crichton. The *New York Times* in one of its heads referred to the play as "a satire on recent phases of social radicalism", and went on to praise it highly as "a fantastic comedy of pure and absolute delight, a masterpiece of the modern English school, beautifully staged, and interpreted with a mingling of sly humor and delicious sentiment . . .". Mr. Gillette, who gave up Hamlet, the critic said, to play the butler, was "as solemn as the ghost of Hamlet's father, and played throughout with exquisite comedy feeling, and in the sentimental passages with his well-loved romantic charm".[4] "Crichton" ran for twenty-six weeks and in the following season went on tour for thirty weeks, including an engagement at the Hollis Theatre in Boston.

From the Lyceum on February 17, 1904, Will wrote "Dr." Fuller that he was grasping at every five minutes to work on a play. This was "Clarice" into which Gillette put some of the May Beecher story and some of his Tryon experiences. In 1904 he started what was to become a more or less annual pilgrimage to Europe in May and June, travelling this time in the Alps and in Wales.

For two benefits in the spring of 1905, Gillette hastily prepared a one-acter called "The Painful Predicament of Sherlock Holmes". First performance was for a Holland benefit on March 24, 1905, at the Metropoliton Opera House, where it was titled "The Frightful Predicament"; the cast of three included Ethel Barrymore as Gwendolyn Cobb. About three weeks later, with the title "The Harrowing Predicament of Sherlock Holmes", it was on the program of the first annual benefit performance in aid of the fund for a larger and better home for the Actors Society of America.

"Clarice" opened with a tryout in Liverpool on September 4, 1905, followed by a London opening at the Duke of York Theatre on September 13. It is interesting that Gillette should have chosen, as he probably did, to have this play produced first in England. The tenor of English criticism is hinted at in the later Boston reviews. Among the English critics, Max Beerbohm singled out an episode in the first act for unfavorable notice. He said that only the previous week he had proclaimed that mimes should never write plays, and expressed regret that Mr. Gillette's play did not allow him to make an exception, but rather to stress this point. For him, Gillette's characters were all puppets. He had to admit that the audience was touched, but as a critic he must report that "Clarice" was little more than a "soap opera" [this phrase not Beerbohm's]. He felt that Gillette himself was the chief mime, and went on:

> I feel that his [Gillette's] favourite portion of "Clarice" is that in which he, solitary on the stage, takes from his pocket the flower that the heroine has given him, and looks at it for a long time, eloquently, and then puts it back in his pocket, and then walks slowly to the window, and thinks, and takes the flower out of his pocket, and looks at it for a very long time, very eloquently, and then restores it to his pocket, and then walks very slowly to his writing-table, and seats himself, and thinks very deeply, and then takes the flower out of his pocket, and after a while, begins to pick it to pieces, petal by petal, after the manner of Marguerite. How long this scene lasted I do not know . . . I was wrapt in contemplation of . . . Mr. Gillette's own innocent pleasure in being able to hold the attention of the audience—his own innocent pride in his own magnetism.[5]

The generally cold reception given to "Clarice" in London may have led to the decision to add "The Painful Predicament" as a curtain-raiser. Charles Chaplin, then about fourteen, was recalled from a Sherlock Holmes company in the provinces to take the role of Billie in the one-act play in London. He later wrote:

> In [the play] Miss Irene Vanbrugh, a remarkably gifted actress, played the madwoman and did all the talking while Holmes [Gillette] just sat and listened. This was [Gillette's] joke on the critics. I [Chaplin] had the opening lines, bursting into Holmes's apartment and holding onto the doors

while the madwoman beats against them outside, and then, while I excitedly try to explain to Holmes the situation, the madwoman bursts in! For twenty minutes she never stops raving incoherently about some case that she wants him to solve, surreptitiously Holmes writes a note, rings a bell, and slips it to me. Later two stalwart men lead the lady off, leaving Holmes and me alone, with me saying "You were right, sir, it was the right asylum."

The critics enjoyed the joke, but the play *Clarissa,* which Gillette wrote for Marie Doro, was a failure. Although they raved about Marie's beauty, they said it was not enough to hold a maudlin play together, so he completed the rest of his season with the revival of *Sherlock Holmes,* in which I was retained for the part of Billie.[6]

Gillette wrote Frohman from the Savoy Hotel on November 5, saying that even if "Holmes" opened well, it would not be likely to last, and suggesting that they play Liverpool for a week, and the following Monday and Tuesday run over to Manchester for a couple of special matinees, and sail Wednesday. He said openly that he wanted to make money on "Holmes" quickly and be through with it—for then.[7]

Gillette had by no means given up on "Clarice". It opened in Boston starting December 25 at the Colonial Theatre. The *Transcript* critic wrote that it was not the play that was a semi-failure in London that Gillette was acting in America. There had been many changes; the piece was stronger and more plausible because of them, and Gillette was credited with having again made use of experience. The faults found in England had been the slow movement of the drama and the improbability of the last scene. In the original last act, Gillette as Dr. Carrington had pretended to take poison in order to show up the deceit of his rival in love. In the new version, Carrington actually took the poison, but his rival, showing his better nature, applied antidotes, at the same time revealing the deceit by which he had attempted to win Carrington's young ward away from him. As rewritten, the scene still seemed unreal, but in performance was more theatrically plausible than had been the original. The pervading improbability, however, remained. Mr. Gillette's abilities had indeed never been strong in the areas of dramatic invention; his skills lay in interpretation, and in "Clarice", these were so well employed that the audience, persuaded to forget improbabilities, showed that it was moved. Gillette was still too fond of what seemed to him meaningful long pauses, and occasionally, his "halting staccato" marred a speech. In general, however, he and his company conveyed a strong impression of living people in a possible situation.[8]

The Boston *Globe* reviewer wrote that Mr. Gillette had created not a comedy, as he called it, but a powerful drama. There was a comic element, to be sure, but the playwright was also capably presenting scenes from the evil side of life. In the first act, between Dr. Carrington and his ward, Clarice, Mr. Gillette had given "as nearly perfect an example of writing as [might] be found in the dramatic output of a decade".[9]

Hartford was as receptive as Boston when Gillette brought "Clarice" to Parsons Theatre on February 10 and 11, 1906. The reviewer wrote that London had seen the play and not liked it, but Boston, "in a mild cultured Bostonese way [had] gone wild over it". He considered that Hartford was subscribing to Boston's view, rather than to London's. "Clarice", he said, had a good proportion of comedy, some melodrama, a clear-cut and pleasant love story, and an averted tragedy—ingredients which were appealing to an audience. He noted especially that, in this play, Mr. Gillette had grown in his ability to make love; this aspect of his acting in previous plays had been weak. Perhaps his present success in expressing tenderness and sincerity could be credited to the presence of Miss Marie Doro, the most appealing leading lady he had ever brought to Hartford.[10]

Before the New York opening of "Clarice", Gillette wrote "Dr." Fuller that he had been in Montreal for the preceding ten days. When the play opened at the Garrick Theatre, the *New York Times* critic labeled Gillette as the author of "a jumble of ineptitude" and found this difficult to explain in a playwright of such skill. He suggested that had Gillette limited himself to one act, he would have had a hit. The plot had a Dr. Carrington relaxing for his health in South Carolina, accompanied by his ward, Clarice. The first act, for Gillette as Carrington, and Marie Doro as Clarice, was a gem. But following this, he had used some rather poor farce and exaggerated melodrama. With a less skilled group of actors, it could quite probably be disastrous.[11]

In the spring of 1907 and again in 1908, Gillette traveled in the Canary Islands, Scotland, Switzerland, and Italy. He was now fifty-five, though somehow (he put the blame on Frohman), his birth date had been allowed to circulate as 1855 rather than 1853. The story was that this happened in connection with a role in a play for which the leading man was described as fifty years of age. Fifty-three, or fifty-five, as the case was, Gillette fully deserved the leisure which he now claimed at least part of the time; yet, in another sense, he could never quite completely give up. This he himself recognised when he wrote to "Dr." Fuller, as he did in December of 1907, that he seemed to be doomed to everlasting work, which, perhaps after all, was best.

One of the most taxing roles of his entire career awaited him in "Samson". The *New York Times* headline of its review read: "Plays Role That Is Out Of His Range". According to the reviewer, the playwright, Henri Bernstein, had become almost as well-known in New York as in Paris the previous season on the strength of a taut little play titled "The Thief". "Samson" was a different piece of work. Perhaps, said the reviewer, all would be well if actors and audience were French. If that were so, Mr. Gillette, " a very good actor within certain very well defined limits", would be a different person. Under the circumstances, New England and French temperaments could not be said to merge. Even so, the utmost in acting skill could make of "Samson" no more than a rather poorly written melodrama. In the plot, a multimillionaire ruins himself to get revenge on a man who has not only tried to steal his wife, but has degraded her. Constance Collier, as the wife, was said to be most effective, with impressive appearance, an excellently trained voice, and a manner of speaking beautifully precise and varied. Mr. Gillette did his best, and conveyed some sense of impending doom, but his big scene was weak. There was nothing about his performance that carried the audience away.[12]

Gertrude Lynch commented in an article in *Theatre* on the rigors of the "Samson" role: "The self torture inflicted by a psychological immersion into the character of Maurice Brachard in 'Samson', during which he had to fight the course of a strong man broken like a reed, so thoroughly wore down William Gillette in this country, as it did Guitry in France, that both actors, by a strange coincidence, finally gave up the same part at almost the same time and for the same reason."[13] Gillette did no acting and wrote no plays for nearly two years after "Samson". He travelled in Germany in

June 1909, and after he came home, wrote "Dr." Fuller from Connecticut that the German doctors had been very good.

The play he worked on next was performed in New York and Boston late in 1910, but it was not successful. New York said of "Electricity": "The audience last night liked it, and applauded many of the lines, and most of the actors." In Boston, however, the reviewer wrote that the audience had come expectant, but were disappointed, even bored. He concluded that playgoers and theatre people had assimilated and outgrown much of what Gillette had to give. He went on:

> The whole theatre as art and institution, had merely gone on, and left Mr. Gillette and his ways standing by the roadside, while we were looking back at him and he was looking forward at us a little desolately. (The thought would come back as he came to bow his thanks to the audience— so grim and grave, so worn and repressed) . . . Mr. Gillette's personages have always seemed made to scale by sand-papered fingers. They were as bloodless as he himself sometimes looks. They lived in a world of their own, which was a world of effect . . . within the theatre.[14]

"Electricity" was Gillette's last significant effort as a playwright. He found himself thinking about retirement.

CHAPTER VIII

"Retirement"

Throughout a long life, William Gillette continued "playing", if not in the theatre, then in some other fashion. His retirement was interrupted by three farewell tours, by ventures in new fields, and by acting again, and again, and yet again. In late 1910, he performed in a repertory program reviving five of his most successful plays, "The Private Secretary", "Held by the Enemy", "Too Much Johnson", "Secret Service", and "Sherlock Holmes". The season opened at the Empire Theatre in New York and closed in April 1911.

One of his new ventures was the lecture platform. His first appearances as a public speaker occurred during the political campaign of 1912. Theodore Roosevelt's Progressive Republican crusade for political and social reform appealed to Gillette, and he volunteered to speak for the Bull Moose cause. The planned itinerary for his tour in October included Baltimore, Washington, Pittsburgh, Penn., Detroit, Chicago, Milwaukee, St. Paul, and Minneapolis. He wrote to author Mark Sullivan for information and material. Sullivan himself had recently undertaken lecturing for the first time and he later wrote Gillette that he had completed his two weeks of lecturing with varying success. On his return to New York, he felt that whether he lectured again or not, he wanted to understand the business better. He asked the help of friends, including William Gillette who had been caught up by the spirit of the Progressive movement and Roosevelt's personality. Gillette, he thought, knew how to speak though his busy career had not allowed him to keep fully informed on public affairs. For instance, he knew little about the objectives of the Progressive Party—the direct primary, direct election of senators, etc. Sullivan instructed Gillette on these points, and Gillette in turn gave Sullivan suggestions about lecturing.[1]

While he was "stumping", Gillette wrote saying that Sullivan was right —people did not "go out" on him—and after the campaign, he told Sullivan that he was glad that he considered his speeches had been of some

Courtesy of The Stowe-Day Foundation

The "Aunt Polly"

Courtesy of The Stowe-Day Foundation

Saloon of the "Aunt Polly"

use. In June 1913 he wrote Sullivan that he was planning some lectures on drama for January and February of the following year, and would like to work in some political talk; he said, in fact, that he was making the lecture tour mainly for this reason.[2]

In more academic vein, Gillette delivered an afternoon speech at graduation exercises of the American Academy of Dramatic Arts in March 1913, setting forth his view of personality as "the most singularly important factor diffusing life into modern stage creations".[3] Later in November of 1913, he was invited to lecture at the fifth joint session of the American Academy of Arts and Letters and the National Institute of Arts and Letters, held in Chicago. For this meeting, Gillette had prepared a piece entitled "The Illusion of the First Time in Acting", an exposition of his ideas on acting and stagecraft, which was later published.

A young reporter named Vincent Starrett was assigned to do a feature story on this conference, and wrote later in his autobiography *Born in a Bookshop: Chapters from the Chicago Renascence* that he thought it was in 1913 that the "Immortals" came to town, meaning by this term the members of the National Institute of Arts and Letters. A program of talks had been arranged for Fullerton Hall at the Art Institute. In anticipation of this event, Starrett was sent to a railroad station to meet the arriving Immortals. Among them, there was only one he wanted greatly to meet, and, as it happened, he did. Pacing through the coaches, he looked into a compartment and there saw a Sherlock Holmes profile outlined against the window. The owner of that profile was gazing out the window, deep in thought, but turned around when Starrett spoke. "Good morning, Mr. Gillette", was Starrett's greeting, and then, "A penny for your thoughts." Gillette's face lighted up. "You would like to know my thoughts, young man?" he said. "I was thinking what a delightful paradox it would be if this train were to roll down the embankment, and all the Immortals were to be killed."[4]

Sometime in 1913, during one of "Aunt Polly's" leisurely cruises on the Connecticut River, Gillette saw the site of his retirement home. He "inherited" his interest and talent in construction and planning from his father, for Francis Gillette's Bloomfield house was built of stone brought from a nearby mountainside. On his Nook Farm property the elder Gillette later built a house of field and cobble stone filled in with gravel, oyster-shell lime, and Rosendale cement. His supervisor of building on the Nook Farm Forest Street house was James Porteus whose sons headed the Porteus-Walker firm which built Will's Connecticut River castle.[5] The term "castle" was a designation Gillette disapproved; he told a newspaper reporter that he had merely laid out a structure that had in it all the things he had always wanted in a house.

In January 1915, Gillette wrote a friend that he was going to build a rough place in which to live, on a hill near Hadlyme, Connecticut.[6] His "rough place" erected between 1914 and 1919 on the loftiest of seven cliffs two hundred feet above sea level, was a reproduction of medieval Rhenish design, constructed of native granite and Southern white oak. Gillette drew the specifications and the builder made only a few changes. The castle contained twenty-four rooms, forty-seven huge doors, and forty-nine types of bolts for which Gillette drew all the sketches and many of which he himself turned out in his own workshop. Stones for the building were carried up by aerial tramway. Gillette named his "rough place" Seventh Sister from the cliff on which it stood. More than one hundred acres of woodland surrounded the castle. Gillette set up residence finally in the 1920's. In a letter to Hamlin Garland written several years later, he said he had been afraid the big, central room of the castle would prove barnlike, but that instead it was cosy, especially in winter with a log fire in the six-foot wide fireplace; for him, cold weather and log fires within far surpassed winter holidays spent in warm climates.[7]

In August 1914, Gillette returned from Europe on the *Baltic*, sailing from Liverpool. He had been at Bad Kissingen, Germany, and was in Paris when war was declared. He reported streets there filled with Americans put out of their hotels and unable to buy food, pathetic sights in London when steamship offices were closed for holidays, August 1–5, and crowds waited in the streets, not knowing what to do.[8] Back in the United States, he appeared as Sherlock Holmes in a benefit for the Belgians organized by Mrs. August Belmont, formerly the actress Eleanor Robson. This "benefit never equaled since" was stage managed by Guthrie McClintic and featured a parade of stars appearing briefly in parts which had made them famous.[9]

Rather suddenly, Gillette was back in the New York theatre world at Frohman's elegant Empire Theatre in a revival of an old play which he had modernized. Sardou's "Diplomacy", with Gillette's changes, opened on October 20, 1914. The *New York Times* critic found evidence of judgment and considerable skill in the carefully wrought and handsomely staged revival being presented at the theatre where the play had been given more than a dozen years ago with William Faversham, Jessie Millward, and Margaret Anglin taking the lead roles. In the revival, the chief actors were William Gillette, Blanche Bates, and Marie Doro, and the old text of the Scott-Stephenson translation had been modernized. All asides and soliloquies had been deleted, and the new play had much to please a 1914 audience. There was an inherent artificiality about the piece, but that it could still be interesting was a credit to the skill and wisdom of the company, particularly to Gillette and Miss Doro. Mr. Gillette, given a warm reception on his return to the stage, acted with the whimsy and something of the gentle protectiveness of his role in "Clarice". This approach was well suited to the part of the good angel in Sardou's play. Miss Doro, lovelier than ever, was most appealing.[10]

Hartford was given two performances of "Diplomacy" in May 1915. The Hartford critic reported a large audience, including hundreds of Mr. Gillette's own friends and admirers. He chose to express some dissatisfaction with the modernized version, saying that a lot of "comedy stuff" had been added. Some of it was effective if one thought of comedy as done merely to make an audience laugh, without any reference to the dramatic place of the lines or scenes. On the other hand, some of the added material was very weak and served only to make the performance last till 11:15 when it should end at 11. Further, the scene of the Beauclerc brothers and Baron Stein had been changed from something clever to a scene of melodrama in order to give the star opportunities for impressive acting. The audience was pleased, however, in spite of changes which many felt did not improve the construction of the play. As to the acting, Mr. Gillette, "tall, thin, intense, and nervously active as ever", played his role consistently along the lines he had laid down at the start of the play.[11]

In November 1914, Gillette, perhaps more at ease than in the hustle-bustle of former years, gave a long interview, speaking his mind freely on the arts of the playwright and the actor. He stressed again the importance of personality. To a question about decadence in the theatre, he replied:

> Well, please don't let's talk about that. The decadent business means livelihood to such a lot of charming and intellectual people that it is a pity to interfere with it in any way. These writers don't do any harm and there is no other variety of talk about the drama that will sell [referring to the critics of decadence]. Nobody on earth can get anything into a newspaper or magazine on the subject of the drama having an upward tendency. At the same time when you meet somebody who begins to talk about decadency to you there is a perfectly safe answer which will end all discussion on the subject and I give you a glad permission to use it. All you have to do is to state to these people that the highest authority in existence has set forth in plain language that the true purpose of the play is to hold the mirror up to nature—meaning, of course, human nature, and this being done at the present day a child in a kindergarten could see why the reflections in that mirror are of the cheapest, meanest, most vulgar and revolting description. You can easily see from this that the reform of the drama must necessarily begin elsewhere than on the stage.[12]

Suddenly Charles Frohman was gone, perishing in the wreck of the *Lusitania* on May 7, 1915. Gillette received the news of his death while in Hartford for performances of "Diplomacy".[13] Frohman's body was washed ashore and Gillette, Faversham, Sothern, Miller, Wilson, and Otis Skinner, with several business associates, "formed the cortege of his pallbearers".[14] Later, there were posthumous Frohman productions of "Sherlock Holmes" and "Secret Service" at the Empire Theatre, and Hartford saw Gillette again in both plays in February of 1916.

In November 1915 Gillette had been elected to the American Academy of Arts and Letters and although uncertain of his worthiness,[15] he nevertheless highly valued the honor. This election complemented his earlier admission to the National Institute of Arts and Letters soon after its organization in 1898.

He corresponded frequently during 1916 with Brander Matthews of Columbia University about the publication of his lecture, "The Illusion of the First Time in Acting", which was to be a part of the second series of *Publications* of the Dramatic Museum of Columbia. In the course of the correspondence, some matter involving unions came up, and Gillette plainly described himself as anti-union and anti-labor leaders, even to the point of disavowing any association with Actors Equity and Authors League if they were to engage in any union activity.[16] Also in 1916, "Sherlock Holmes" was made into a film. Gillette and Arthur Bertelet directed the 7-reel Essanay film with Gillette as Sherlock, Ernest Maupain as Moriarty, and Edward Fielding as Dr. Watson. Gillette's personality did not come through well on the screen, and there were no more film ventures.

Another play was in rehearsal for Broadway during this period, a light comedy written by Clare Kummer who was a relative of Gillette. "A Successful Calamity", opening at the Booth Theatre on February 5, 1917, cast Gillette as a weary multimillionaire who pretended to be ruined in order to bring his self-centered and reckless family into line. Critical notice was thoroughly favorable, with the play considered "a triumph" for Clare Kummer and for the producer, Arthur Hopkins. Mr. Gillette, in the lead role, was thought to be looking unusually fit. His role suited him well and offered the opportunity of expressing the tender, protective quality reminiscent of the part he had played in "Clarice". As the critic put it, Mr. Gillette was always "benignly quizzical". In this production, he was one of an excellent company. "A Successful Calamity" had no real starring role, whereas the Frohman productions had often featured a well-known star surrounded by rather mediocre supporting actors.[17] "A Successful Calamity" went on a road tour after a long run in New York.

Another Barrie play went into rehearsal in the fall of 1918, entitled "Dear Brutus", in which the role of the dream daughter was taken by a young actress named Helen Hayes. Gillette had met Helen some time before when she had appeared for a part in an earlier play and at a time when it seemed she might have to resign herself to playing children's roles. Gillette had said to her then, "I hear you are a great actress, but I am afraid I am too tall to play opposite you. I'll have a grand part for you some day, I'm sure."

During rehearsals of "Dear Brutus", Helen suffered from double direction, since Gillette changed most of the suggestions of the director, Iden Paine. At Atlantic City where "Dear Brutus" played for a week starting December 11, with simultaneous rehearsals, Helen seemed to be giving a sort of composite performance and felt that it was poor. Gillette contrived to dispel most of her misgivings by meeting her as she returned from a long walk with her mother and saying, "I have been waiting for you, 'Dream Daughter', to give you a message from Mr. Hayman. He said to tell you he was prouder than ever of his great little leading lady."

From Atlantic City, the company went to Washington for a week. Gillette "sensed that Helen was worried, so he would send his valet with notes to [her] dressing room, saying he had something very important to talk to her about, and would she stop at his room before the second act. It was never anything important and he would never mention the play. He would have a funny little toy or novelty . . . or he would tell her of some awful mishap he had had when he first came on the stage. By the time the curtain would go up on the second act, their act, they would make their entrance in gales of real laughter." On opening night, in New York, December 23, Helen received the following letter from Mr. Gillette:

> Dream of My Life:
> It is important that I come up at once. It will be impossible for me to play the second act unless you let me come for my mind would be distracted and harassed. It must be *at rest*. Make it so by saying to the Japanese one that I may come for a moment. I am relying on you for this.
> Your Hallucination Daddy.

He climbed four flights to her dressing room just to tell her that she would be "magnificent".[18]

Of the resulting performance John Corbin wrote for the *New York Times:* "The scene in the enchanted forest between the happy if commonplace artist and his adorable daughter, who might have been, had all the spiritual comprehension and the wistful beauty in affection of Barrie at his best. Mr. Gillette has never been more humanly gracious and delicately real; and he is admirably seconded by Helen Hays [sic] whose little Margaret is a wonderful blending of dream beauty and girlish actuality."[19]

Helen's fourth floor dressing room became headquarters for a smoking circle of actors and actresses at intermission between the first and second acts. Gillette at first did not join them, but then asked if he might. He would "come bounding up those iron stairs with the most amazing agility

Courtesy of Theatre Collection, The New York Public Library, Astor, Lenox and Tilden Foundations

Helen Hayes and William Gillette in "Dear Brutus"

for one in his sixties".[18] Over the years Gillette had found many May Beechers, and Helen Hayes was yet another young woman to cherish and another young actress whose career he could foster. He was much put out when she left the cast to join a repertory company for six weeks.

At least twice during 1918 and 1919, the war which was going on impinged on Gillette's life. He was asked to contribute an article to an American Academy of Arts and Letters volume entitled *The World War: Utterances Concerning its Issues and Conduct by Members of the American Academy of Arts and Letters*. Gillette had been reluctant to express himself on this subject,[20] but finally put his mind to it and produced a brief statement. On the other occasion, his manager had received and transmitted to him an appeal that speakers be recruited to talk in schools, theatres, etc., on thrift through savings bonds. This kindled Gillette's wrath, for he felt that the theatre belonged exclusively to the players and the performance for which it had been booked.[21] The young Gillette who gave his high school prize essay on "Opposition" had become a man who found himself now and then at odds with the world.

At the end of May 1919, George Warner died at Tryon. His wife, Gillette's sister, Lilly Gillette Warner, had died in 1915. With both parents gone, their daughter Margaret, who was not well, became one of Gillette's responsibilities.

In the fall of 1919, Gillette began an extended tour in "Dear Brutus", playing Springfield, Massachusetts, Boston, Philadelphia, Chicago, Detroit, Wilkes-Barre, and other cities. The engagements ran into the spring of 1920. One of the cast during this tour was a coming actress named Judith Anderson. Her role was not that of the dream daughter, but of Joanna Trout, one of the two unmarried ladies in Barrie's comedy fantasy of a Midsummer Eve's "second chance".[22]

Gillette wrote another play called "The Dream Maker" which, on its New York opening on November 21, 1921, was reviewed by a young drama critic named Alexander Woollcott who wrote that Gillette was greeted on his return to the Empire Theatre by a huge, affectionate, and benevolent audience. The spectators had probably expected from the title something of a sentimental fantasy. "The Dream Maker" was instead an entertaining melodrama, the sort of piece that might be expected from a retired playwright who had made money and had a great deal of fun with "Sherlock Holmes". Woollcott found in the play and the actor a Sherlock Holmes grown old and a William Gillette grown older. The years had not, however, lessened the appeal and skill of Gillette's plays and acting. He found in William Gillette an odd quality which almost prepared one for the thwarting of the three blackmailers by the device of making them sick at their stomachs. The "nausea motif", he thought, was novel in this type of melodrama.[23]

By the early 1920's, Gillette was setting up a kind of residence at his castle. In March 1922 he failed to persuade the Board of Relief of the Town of Lyme, Connecticut, to grant him a reduction in the tax listing of his castle and grounds at Hadlyme. The board listed the property as worth $58,300 for taxable purposes, while Gillette said it should be listed as worth not more than $22,350. The castle, according to a 1922 newspaper story, had been under construction for six years and was still not finished, though Gillette could spend summers there with his Japanese cook and cat. He appealed to the Superior Court from the Tax Board's finding.[24] In October 1922 he valued the castle at $21,050 for the grand list, but the assessor raised the figure to $71,000, and the Board of Relief reduced it to $69,000.[25] In addition to these troubles, his boat, "Aunt Polly", had begun to leak. He therefore planned to take her from the river, build a concrete foundation under her, and turn her into a garden house.[26]

There was another farewell tour, and revivals, in 1922–23, with "Dear Brutus", "Sherlock", and "Private Secretary" being offered. At this time, he wrote often to Amelia Watson who was then living in Tryon. A letter of May 1923 indicates that he was trying to dispose of his Tryon property. He was still buying Amelia's water colors, and told her that he was having a place made for paintings in the castle—he would put all of hers there— a roomful, with the two sketchbooks on a table.[27]

Gillette wrote Alexander Woollcott that writers who had referred to his "fastness" on a cliff above the Connecticut River should have made it his "slowness".[28] The slowness had come gradually. Only a few years before, Gillette was riding a motorcycle around Hadlyme. One day in 1918, as he was coming down to the ferry landing, the braking mechanism on the cycle failed, and Gillette, on the vehicle, shot off the landing into the

Connecticut River. He swam ashore, and as he was already dripping wet, he proposed diving down to put a line on the cycle, but was dissuaded by the ferryboat men.[29]

But there *was* more and more leisure in these years—enough even for writing a novel. Harper and Brothers published *The Astounding Crime on Torrington Road* in 1927. His Torrington Road was in Massachusetts, not in Connecticut. An imaginative reader could find in the book some of the elements of the Gillette life story transformed into a new thing of Gillette's creation: the young inventor—Will Gillette; the poignant and interrupted romance—Gillette's own; the kindly old Mrs. Temple—Aunt Polly of North Carolina. Notices on the whole were favorable:

> *The Springfield Republican:* The crime is the supposed murder of a young inventor by schemers trying to rob him of the child of his brain.
> *Saturday Review:* quite as interesting as a writer as he is skilful and convincing as an actor.
> Will Cuppy in *New York Herald Tribune Books:* Sacrificial love, a thread of spiritism, and something entirely new in grewsome takings-off are among the treats, while a novel narrative method adds its bit.
> *Boston Transcript:* In writing this clever tale of adventure and crime, Mr. Gillette has several qualities entirely absent from the professional detective story author. In the first place, he uses his own style, an original one. Secondly, he invents complications in his plot as he goes along. Thirdly, he shows at moments a deep interest in making his characters real people.
> *New York Times:* a baffling and, on the whole, satisfactory piece of mystery writing.

In addition to creative writing, Gillette was carrying on a correspondence with the theatrical producer, George Crouse Tyler, one which grew in volume in 1928. It had to do with a nation-wide revival tour of "Sherlock Holmes".

CHAPTER IX

Honors and last farewells

Gillette's Tryon place was much on his mind in 1928 and he corresponded frequently with Amelia Watson. In January just before a trip abroad, he wrote her from Hadlyme to report having heard that Margaret Warner's things were being used for the tea room in Tryon. He commiserated with her on how much trouble they were all having about "ten cents worth of stuff". He would be back, he said, on April 16. The trip was chiefly to see Margaret in Paris and to visit friends in London. On his return he wrote again several times, first to thank Amelia and a friend for their help in rescuing Margaret's things and then to express relief that the property had been purchased. In July he wrote Miss Watson asking her to send a few lines to Margaret who was in Switzerland for her health and as he put it, "living on letters"; he cautioned her to give no indication that she knew Margaret's actual condition.[1]

Early in 1928, George Crouse Tyler began to sound Gillette out on the subject of a revival tour of "Sherlock Holmes". Gillette wrote him from London that it would take a good deal of persuading to make him do it—he had done it so much that the prospect was wearisome and there was the added deterrent of possible adverse criticism, a real hazard, to his present way of thinking.[2] Softening somewhat, he replied to a Tyler letter that he was disappointed that the production apparently could not have an all-star cast; he did not think he alone had enough drawing power to get them more than a middling volume of business. The discussion went on into 1929. By June of that year, he had given his consent, but in a "P.S." to that letter he raised with Tyler the question whether, as a non-member of Equity, he would be allowed to act. Tyler managed things, and a letter from the Executive Secretary of Actors Equity stated that the Council would grant Mr. Gillette a special exemption in view of his outstanding service in the theatre. This episode recalled for Gillette the early days of the organization of Equity and an opposition group, with neither of which had he associated himself. In mid-July Gillette reflected a bit on his age, his

Courtesy of The State Park and Forest Commission   The big fireplace, Gillette Castle

occasional "off" days, and the fact that Sherlock was a hard part. He told Tyler that such thoughts brought him near to saying "No" to the whole thing. By August, however, they were discussing routes; Tyler was planning a tour to extend into spring of 1930, which left Gillette somewhat aghast, fearing he would be worn out after twenty weeks and remembering that thirty weeks of "Sherlock", even when he was young and well, had run his weight down from 160 to 130 pounds.

On August 13 the *New York Times* reported that William Gillette was to return to the stage for a farewell tour in "Sherlock Holmes", to begin at Ford's Theatre in Baltimore. The story said the producer had negotiated with Gillette for the tour for nearly a year, and since he did not belong to either Actors Equity or Actors Fidelity League, the Council of Equity had suspended its rules and granted Mr. Gillette an exemption.[3]

Gillette and Tyler next turned their attention to casting. For the part of Moriarty, Gillette said they needed someone terrifyingly strong, dangerous, and convincingly murderous—a cold, hard, venomous chap. Moriarty's henchmen must be of large physique—Holmes should not be facing midgets in the gas chamber. He kept emphasizing what he called the "dangerous" or evil atmosphere it was necessary to sustain, saying if Sherlock was in no danger, the bottom was knocked out of the piece.

Gillette took a brief trip to Canada, and on his return wrote to his long-time associate, William Postance, urging that he not allow personal enmity toward Miltern to stand in the way of his serving the upcoming production. Not least among Gillette's reasons for wanting Postance as his Sid Prince were their long association and personal friendship, and he acknowledged the assistance Postance had given in the writing of the "Sherlock" play. About the feminine role of Alice Faulkner, Gillette wrote Tyler in October that if he got a twenty-eight or thirty year old woman, her situation would seem so absurd that it would evoke laughter; they must have a helpless young thing—*very* young. He hoped Tyler could find a young girl, not the product of elocution lessons, and one as attractive as possible.

The farewell tour opened in Springfield, Massachusetts, on November 15, 1929. The *New York Times* reported on November 18 that Gillette's farewell tour would open in Boston that day for one week. There had been letters of congratulation from former President Coolidge, Booth Tarkington, Ruth McCormick, Mrs. Corinne Roosevelt Robinson, and President Emeritus Arthur T. Hadley of Yale.[4] Sir Arthur Conan Doyle wrote: "Your return in 'Sherlock Holmes' is, of course, a source of personal gratification, my only complaint being that you make the poor hero of the anemic printed page a very limp object as compared with the glamour of your own personality."

In New York, Gillette received "one of the ovations of the year as he stepped out upon the stage in his old role—tall, austere, impassive, soft-spoken, magnetic".[5] J. Brooks Atkinson wrote in the *New York Times* that some of the tricks of "Sherlock" were barefaced: "You see thru them and beyond, but you can still enjoy it. The stage business and manner of acting are dated, but it doesn't matter." He summed it up as an "evening of affectionate enjoyment". At the conclusion of the play, William Lyon Phelps conferred on Gillette an honorary M.A.—Master of Acting.[6]

"Sherlock" went to Washington early in 1930. Gillette was a guest at the White House for luncheon, with Clayton Hamilton, the playwright. In addition to this entertainment by President Hoover, Vice President Curtis gave a dinner at the Mayflower Hotel with reception later at the Congressional Club.

Hartford had three night performances and one matinee, February 10–12, 1930. Walter Brown in the *Hartford Courant* reported Gillette as "looking very young indeed, and no slowness of motion betrayed the fact that the years have passed . . . The voice, which was never heavy nor strained in use, was the same as ever—low, incisive when action demanded, seemingly hesitant at times with the odd impression that the lines were being given for the first time—which is one of the finest arts of the actor . . . ."[7] On February 11, Gillette was the guest of honor at a public testimonial luncheon given for him at the Hartford Club. He was introduced by Attorney Arthur L. Shipman, and in the audience were two of his cousins, Miss Katherine S. Day and Joseph K. Hooker.[8] A painting by the Connecticut artist William Gedney Bunce, entitled "Venetian Boats", was presented to Gillette.

There was a testimonial dinner at the Lotos Club, in New York, attended by more than three hundred members and guests, with Dr. Nicholas Murray Butler as toastmaster. The 1929–30 tour ended at Princeton University on May 12, 1930.[9]

On June 3 Gillette began making the rounds of eastern colleges, collecting honorary degrees. His first was received from Columbia, an LL.D. On June 16 he was given an M.A. by Trinity College, on June 17 an LL.D. by Dartmouth, and on June 19 an M.A. by Yale.

On June 11 from Hadlyme he ordered gas cylinders for a locomotive to run on his property and the *New York Times* on August 20 reported on his new diversion of miniature railroading, with track laid through the castle woods.

Already in March of 1930, Tyler and he had begun correspondence about the next leg of the tour. On March 20, Gillette wrote that there was no chance of his going out next season unless he could have a short run of ten or eleven weeks without a lot of small-town stands. In August they were discussing it again, and again Gillette protested dragging the play to small unresponsive audiences. On September 1, he wrote Tyler of having to be in Hartford every afternoon for observation and treatment of a weakened heart. He referred again to unresponsive houses, saying they had had them in Buffalo, Milwaukee, St. Louis, Louisville, Cleveland, Detroit, Cincinnati, and Pittsburgh. It was depression time; nobody had money for theatre except the upper crusters and Tyler must know the type of audience they made; besides, the strain and work of acting under those conditions was almost intolerable. Again in a September 6 letter he returned to the theme of cold audiences which they had in almost all the towns after Newark, except Hartford and New Haven. Indianapolis and Princeton were the only exceptions in the strain of the last half of the season, and the only places where enthusiastic and demonstrative people had come to the theatre. He told Tyler he was very fond of him and that some day he would be very glad he'd made him postpone the West Coast trip. On November 26, he wrote that he was praying to whatever ruled the universe that the business situation would improve enough to make it possible for the delayed tour of "Sherlock" to do extremely well.

The October 19 *New York Times* reported that Gillette was to make his radio debut as Sherlock Holmes over WEAF. According to the reviewer in the *Times* of the following Sunday: "Sherlock Holmes underwent his third transformation when William Gillette who gave him flesh and blood on the stage, breathed his voice over the radio last Monday night." The voice, he wrote, was "clear, precise, vibrant". The Holmes exploit chosen for this debut was "The Adventure of the Speckled Band."[10]

Margaret Warner died on February 23, 1931 and was buried at Farmington, Connecticut. Gillette wrote Amelia Watson from Hadlyme, reporting this and telling her that it was delightful to remember old days in Tryon when it was not too painful.

"The Admirable Crichton" was revived on March 9, 1931 in New York, and after the performance, Gillette, recalling his 1903 success, shared the applause with the stars, Walter Hampden and Fay Bainter. A

Courtesy of The Stowe-Day Foundation

Gillette in the cab of one of his locomotives

Courtesy of The Stowe-Day Foundation

Gillette with railroad engineers

letter from James Barrie was read, actually a playlet, in which the characters were Gillette, Hampden, and members of the cast.

Resuming his correspondence with Tyler in June 1931, Gillette went back to the matter of one-night stands, saying he found it worrisome, with the need of hurrying the play on, a late curtain, performance lasting till 11:30 or 12, and the same thing over again the next night. In a "P.S." he asked whether Tyler had found him a wonderful Alice as his leading lady.

On November 11, Gillette was the recipient of the gold medal of the National Institute of Arts and Letters for his work as a dramatic author. The medal was awarded once in a decade, and previous recipients in the theatre had been Augustus Thomas in 1913 and Eugene O'Neill in 1922.[11]

In early December Gillette expressed to Tyler his chagrin at not having had the privilege of seeing all the candidates for parts beforehand and personally making the selection. It was the first time in his life, he said, that this had happened, and recalled that Tyler had granted him this privilege in October 1929. He graciously conceded that its absence this time was undoubtedly the result of a good intention to spare him effort. Four days later he wrote to say that he was coming down to meet the cast.

Before the beginning of the second half of the farewell tour of "Sherlock", Gillette received a letter signed by ten or more educators in the Boston area asking him to start the tour in Boston which had lost the second of two weeks promised in 1929 because he was then needed for a New York performance.[12] The request was granted and "Sherlock" played Boston from December 28, 1931 to January 2, 1932. The second tour was brief, however, ending with a performance in Wilmington, Delaware, on March 19, 1932.

Gillette wrote Tyler in May that he had been in New York a few days on his return from an ocean trip which he had so longed for that he very nearly boarded the first ship going out. He was having financial problems —trying to settle his accounts for the "Sherlock" tour and helping to support various relatives. In a later May letter he said the depression would right itself if the United States had a Mussolini to get Congress out of Washington and keep it out. Things were running so close financially, that he even thought of trying to sell his Hadlyme property.

From Hadlyme he wrote on August 9 to Eleanor Robson Belmont, former actress, who, knowing of his railroad, had asked whether he knew about the underground transportation system for Congressmen in Washington. He replied that the Congress conveyance was nothing but a trolley line put out of sight, with no locomotive, steam boiler, pumps, whistle, air brakes, pressure gauge, throttle valve, fire box, water gauge, smoke stack, safety valve, etc., etc. In fact, it ran by a broomstick held up in the air. He apologized for boring her, but said it had to be stated in defense of his rolling stock.[13]

Life at the castle was pleasant. Guthrie Burton, Richard's second wife, recalled spending some time every September at the castle, enjoying with her husband the company of Gillette and his brother-in-law, Hall Cowan, Helen's much younger half-brother, and Hall's wife, who lived at the castle with him in his later years. Gillette and the Cowans, she said, were devoted to one another, and in the evening, the huge fireplace would be ablaze, lights low, and hours would be spent in delightful reminiscence. She remembered that Winchell Smith, playwright, drove down from Farmington for lunch or the evening. Dr. Albert Einstein and his wife came for a brief visit which included a ride on the little railroad. Einstein took great pleasure in the experience. Gillette, Mrs. Burton said, loved to be at the throttle in his railroading costume, and skillfully drove the locomotive and its two passenger cars over the winding track through the woods with occasional glimpses of the river. Y. Osaki, Gillette's former dresser and valet, was still a valued member of his household; he was of a family prominent in Japan, and Gillette treated him with formality and respect, and each night at midnight, he and Osaki spent half an hour in conversation.[14]

A sad event of late 1932 was the burning of "Aunt Polly". Various stories about the happening circulated in the valley. A notice finally appeared in one of the local newspapers:

A CARD OF THANKS

As it is impossible to answer so many letters personally, I am venturing to express publicly my sincere appreciation of the kindness of those in this vicinity and also throughout the United States and abroad who have written me sympathetically about the burning of my boat "The Aunt Polly".

Also, I will take this opportunity to say that the report circulated by dear friends in Hadlyme to the effect that I set fire to the yacht myself in order to get the insurance on her, is a trifle incorrect, owing to the fact that there was no insurance. I did not think of it in time.

WILLIAM GILLETTE

Hadlyme, Conn., Feb. 4, 1933

Gillette celebrated his eightieth birthday, in the proper year—1933, and in New York City. On the occasion, he received from the Hartford Wheel Club a congratulatory telegram composed by Lucius H. Elmer, a charter member of the old cycling organization of which Gillette had been an honorary member for six years. The felicitation read: "One hundred and fifty veteran Wheel Club members join me in congratulating you on your 80th birthday. All Hartford is proud of you and your accomplishments of the past. If America had more men of your type, it would be a better place to live in. We expect you at the next reunion September 21, looking as youthful as ever. Our prayer is that you can continue to be with us for many years to come."[15]

In a letter of July 7, 1934, Gillette told Alexander Woollcott that he must soon go out to the coast on a business trip from which he probably would not return until late August. He congratulated Woollcott on being in an exquisite region—Vermont.[16] On November 25, he accepted an invitation to attend the Sherlock Holmes dinner of the Baker Street Irregulars in New York. Vincent Starrett recalled the occasion in his autobiography *Born in a Bookshop: Chapters from the Chicago Renascence:*

> I reached the dining room precisely at six-thirty, thanks to Woollcott's uncanny timing, was greeted by Elmer Davis with a highball in each hand, and seated myself at the table about seven-thirty, where I snoozed gently between Morley and Frederic Dorr Steele—slightly supported by Steele—until perhaps nine. At this time there was a commotion in the corridor and I came out of my coma with what is described by novelists as a start. The door was flung swiftly open and in the aperture stood Sherlock Holmes himself...
>
> It was Gillette, of course, and when the uproar for him had died away the dinner went forward as planned.[17]

In June 1935, Gillette answered the letter of Perriton Maxwell who had proposed a weekly radio play series. He rejected the idea, saying it was beyond anything he could undertake. Mark Twain sketches were being considered as the material, moreover, and Gillette considered them unsuitable.[18]

Ward Morehouse visited Gillette at the castle in the early fall of 1935, and was given a ride at twenty miles an hour on the railroad. He found Gillette "alert, vigorous, and courtly", retaining "all his humor and charm". For the locomotive he wore overalls and cap, but an hour later, "wearing black, a gold watch chain looped across his waistcoat, he came silently down the balcony stairway . . . dignified, calm, erect, commanding. And as he spoke—laconic, crisp, crackling, shrill—I felt that Mr. Holmes had slipped into this great stone house."[19]

In November of that year, Gillette appeared in a tabloid version of "Sherlock Holmes" on WABC's Radio Theatre. The *New York Times* critic reported that Gillette "observed vocal nuances" and seemed to improvise.[20]

For the last time, in 1936, Gillette returned to the stage. Among his persuaders, according to the *New York Times* story, were John Golden, Clayton Hamilton, Roy Howard, Grover Whalen, Nicholas Murray Butler, Bernard Baruch, and William Lyon Phelps. The vehicle was to be Austin Strong's "Three Wise Fools", a revival, with Gillette as the irascible, yet kindly Theodore Findley; he was supported by James Kirkwood, Charles Coburn, and—for the first performances—Mary Rogers, daughter of Will Rogers. It was a brief road tour opening at the Shubert Theatre in Newark on January 13, 1936, proceeding to Philadelphia, Washington, Boston, Springfield, and Hartford, and winding up at the Golden Theatre in New York.

The *Newark Star Eagle* reporter found that Mr. Gillette at eighty-three remained "an electric personality that [knew] every trick in the footlight handbook" and "riveted the attention of the spectators by his manner in arranging cards for a solitaire game, in lighting a cigar, or by handing the heroine a handkerchief. Under-acting [was] the keynote for his special magic." The *Boston Globe* of February 11, 1936 said: "It would well repay the best of our actors to carefully study the illusively effective naturalness of his acting." Betty Hynes in a Washington newspaper review of the play wrote: "At the end it was an aching futility to try to convey to him

Courtesy of The State Park and Forest Commission

Gillette Castle, Hadlyme

how really remarkable his performance was. His pointing of lines, his splendid delivery that without raising his still magnificent voice, never lost a word. A great object lesson for aspiring actors to see and hear, and for mumblers to remember." The *Washington Evening Star* critic advised the younger Garbos and Gables to go to the National Theatre and learn "what otherwise they may never even suspect". After the Hartford performance on February 27, 1936, T. H. Parker wrote in the *Courant* that he had watched Gillette "pursue his polished and easy way through 'Three Wise Fools' ". In one of his rare curtain speeches from the stage of Bushnell Hall, Gillette said: "I should apologize for being here, but I am a man among Yankees, and they take promises with a grain of salt . . . You men who follow horse racing will know what I mean. I'm not running against anyone, they're merely letting me trot around the track."

Following the final curtain in New York in early March, the company and invited guests gathered backstage to extend tributes to the veteran actor whose career spanned more than sixty years. The guests included May Irwin, Cecilia Loftus, Lenore Ulric, Frank McIntyre, Edmund Breese, George M. Cohan, Helen Hayes, Florence Reed, and Fritzi Scheff. Good wishes came from John Golden in Florida via radio.

Gillette's performance in Hartford was his farewell to his home town, as was an appearance on the stage of Hartford High School at about the same period, when he spoke to the students as an "old grad" recalling the past.[21]

Gillette was brought to Hartford in December 1936 to enter Hartford Hospital for treatment of a bad cold from which he had suffered for more than two months. Although the papers reported him as eighty-one, he *was* now eighty-three. He was made to rest and was given two blood transfusions, and by December 16 was reported exercising daily in the corridors and gaining weight. He returned to Hadlyme, but entered the hospital again in early April and steadily lost strength. The final curtain came for him on April 29, 1937. In accordance with his wishes, there was no funeral service. A burial service was conducted at the grave in Riverside Cemetery in Farmington, and he was laid to rest beside Helen in the Gillette family plot.

Gillette's lifelong friend, Richard Burton, commemorated their friendship and paid tribute to the man William Gillette in a poem written not long after his death:

ASLEEP AT FARMINGTON

Sleep well, dear Lad—yes still to me
You are a lad of eighty-three!
Of all the lads beneath the sun
The most to be depended on.
Beneath the sun, beneath the sod
What matters it? Leave that to God.

Sleep well at Farmington, old town
Of peace and beauty. To lie down
In such a spot, for quiet rest
Surely were good, surely were best
Of fates for any man whose sleep
Would be content and long and deep.
Your kin are there beside you, so
Whether hot sun or winter snow
Visit the place there shall abide
A sense of kindred at your side;
Whate'er the legend cut in stone,
You are not lost or left alone;

And though no word escape your lip
Tranquil in that ripe fellowship
Yours is a happy end ——— 'Tis we
Who mourn you, lack felicity!

The last will and testament of William Gillette was characteristic of the man. He wrote, in part:

> That the property at Hadlyme, Conn., which has been my home for fifteen years, and upon which I have built a house and other structures together with a narrow-gauge railway of approximately three miles in length, railway shops, and a roundhouse for the two locomotives (one electric storage batteries, the other steam), and for the several passenger cars of the road; and throughout the place, numerous paths, ponds and bridges, etc., may become the possession of a person or persons fitted by nature to appreciate not only the extraordinary natural beauty of the situation and its surroundings, but more especially the mechanical features connected with it and established upon it during the time that I have occupied it as a home.

I would consider it more than unfortunate for me—should I find myself doomed, after death, to a continued consciousness of the behavior of mankind on this planet—to discover that the stone walls and towers and fireplaces of my home, founded at every point on the solid rock of Connecticut; that my railway line with its bridges, trestles, tunnels through solid rock, mid stone culverts and underpasses, all built in every particular for performance (so far as there is such a thing); that my locomotives and cars, constructed on the safest and most efficient mechanical principles; that these and many other things of a like nature should reveal themselves to me as in the possession of some blithering saphead who had no conception of where he is or with what surrounded.

For this reason I am hoping that my executors, in disposing of this property, as they will be obliged to do, will exercise discrimination in carrying out my earnest wish. I will say here that if I were alive and conducting the sale myself the price for the property would, if necessary, be considerably less to an appreciative customer in the way indicated than to one who had no capacity whatever for mechanical satisfaction.

Gillette's beloved castle and Hadlyme property were sold at auction on October 15, 1938 for $35,000 to Louis Schlesinger, Newark real estate broker. Schlesinger's bid was cancelled by Gillette's executors, Joseph K. Hooker and the First National Bank of Hartford, in accordance with a section of the terms of sale which stated that the bid was being made subject to confirmation by the executors who had the right to refuse acceptance of the bid. The State of Connecticut purchased the castle and surrounding property in 1943. In an address given at the opening of the castle on October 7, 1944, Henry A. Perkins of Hartford said: "When other people were building Colonial villas at the seashore, Gillette built a Rhine castle on the Connecticut. . . . This 'Castle' is a tangible expression of [his] personality, winning, whimsical, aloof, and will long stand as his most perfect memorial, when his plays and his roles in them have been forgotten."[22] The railroad, cherished creation of Gillette's retirement, was sold to an amusement park in Southington, Connecticut, where it still delights visitors with its run around the shores of Lake Compounce.

CHAPTER X

As they saw him and as he was

To people in the theatre and business world, to audiences and acquaintances, William Gillette seemed aloof, austere, dryly droll, eccentric, escapist, gay and charming in conversation. Others recalled him as a gentleman, handsome, impishly humorous, independent, laconic, a ladies' man, meticulous, a practical joker, reserved, scholarly-looking, self-sufficient, taciturn, tall, and sometimes testy. Mark Twain's maid, Katy Leary, prefigured Gillette's role as matinee idol when she said she thought him "the handsomest man" she had ever looked at, and that she was "just crazy about him".[1]

If the young Will was handsome, the mature and elderly Will were handsome, too. During the tour of "Three Wise Fools", Nelson R. Bell wrote in the *Washington Post* of February 4, 1936, that Gillette stood "6 feet 3 inches tall". Leo Carroll, of the theatre world, recalled Gillette about a year before his death as "handsome as ever" and "standing like a lance, tall and distinguished".[2] Gillette was proud of his mobility in later life, taking time to write on a rotogravure picture of J. P. Sousa who was celebrating *his* 77th birthday: "I've got the best of *him* anyway—at 77 he has to be helped around."[3] William Winter in his *New York Herald Tribune* obituary of Gillette in 1937 remembered him as "tall, lithe, muscular, expeditious, icy, and indomitable . . . clerical in aspect and crisp in vocalism".

Gillette's image on Broadway must have verged on the patrician. The actress Billie Burke called him "the great aristocrat of the theatre".[4] Yet Rennold Wolf in 1907 described a Gillette "painfully modest", detesting a crowd, waiting until most of the guests had left a public dining room before entering, and talking walks very late at night.[5] Drama critic Ward Morehouse wrote that Gillette "had a special police permit to take his constitutional in Central Park" at hours after it was closed to the public.[6] He cannot, therefore, have been hail-fellow-well-met with the public or even with the majority of theatre people.

Courtesy of The Connecticut Historical Society

William Gillette

The great theatre manager, Daniel Frohman, thought that social life was not a source of pleasure to Gillette and that he preferred to be alone or with a few close friends.[7] Rennold Wolf wrote that he was "a very good friend to a small coterie of friends".[5] Henry A. Perkins, a later Nook Farm resident, who drew one of the best of all word portraits of Gillette, said that he "had a wide acquaintance, but a very limited circle of close friends", that his close friends in New York were largely in "the Profession", and that he also had a group of friends in England who entertained him royally.[8]

Interviewers he turned away regularly, with a few notable exceptions, particularly the representatives of magazines around the turn of the century and the reporter who saw him for the *New York Times* in November 1914. Much more typical is his reply to the person who approached him at the Plaza Hotel in July 1935 and asked if he might speak to him, and in particular about his birthday: " 'Oh, hell, no.' And he was gone down the hall with his bags. 'I have never given an interview and it is too late to start now.' "[9]

Will had indeed a complex personality. W. H. Briggs of Harper & Brothers touched upon one phase of its ambiguities when he wrote Gillette that, in the matter of the novel he was having published, he [Gillette] had "shunned the extremes of publicity religiously while at the very same time he was making legitimate use of it".[10]

Amy Leslie, theatre critic of the *Chicago Daily News,* had a conversation with Gillette in late 1897, in which he talked of cycling and his desire for a farm with one hen, a cat, a "perennial pup", and some radishes or whatever grew easily in a back yard. Here spoke the perennial lad, Gillette. But they talked of many other things, and as Miss Leslie listened, she found that Gillette's appeal lay in a complete sincerity combined with a gentle cynicism. She described him as "slender and ungraceful in a gentlemanly attractive fashion, sudden and eccentric in gesture, and infinitely slow in everything but thought, wit and argument". His face, she wrote, was "a map of joys and griefs . . . still retaining so adorable a touch of unsullied youth as to give it a beauty and purity almost feminine". He hinted at lost illusions, but carried on "a mischievous banter shot at himself and his whims, his fatigue and his fate. There [was] always a quizzical sparkle of laughter in his eyes unless they [were] seriously convincing a listener . . . Then they [were] very blue and deep, full of solemn brightness and magnetism." Gillette, she said, was "so temperamental and unusual that it [was] difficult to decide whether his fine brain and superb intellectual balance or his brilliant wit, his kindliness and general companionable fitness [were] the enticing elements in his personality." Beneath all his light conversation, quick wit, and flow of compliment and foolery, "his fantastic notions of things and his unrelenting satire", she found a deep sympathy and a profound intellect "so vividly singular and powerful that there [was] almost intimidation in the discovery of them".[11]

Burns Mantle, drama critic, wrote in the *New York Daily News* for May 2, 1937, following Gillette's death, that he had "frequently sought a complete escape from life". This seems to have been true: when his wife's and mother's deaths, financial reverses, and the failure of "Ninety Days" weakened his health, he escaped to Tryon and other remote places; periodically he escaped from the theatre world in travel, in Hartford, and on his boat; the castle, scene of most of his retirement, was also an escape of sorts. His neighbor, Alice Hamilton, gave a glimpse of the escapist Gillette, speaking of him first as "the most beloved outsider who ever came to Hadlyme", though he did not consider himself as such, feeling instead that he did belong, loved the neighborhood, and was loved in return. When the Hamiltons first came, Gillette was living on "Aunt Polly" while the castle was being built. Miss Hamilton remembered Gillette as a person of unusual charm, with a winning quality, and at the same time a shyness which seemed amusing in an actor. He did not call unless he knew that the Hamiltons were alone, but if they invited him to a large party, he would come and "make himself the center of it". He was unusually hospitable, but quite averse to being taken by surprise. She saw him more than once dodge behind a tree when she encountered him unexpectedly while walking through the castle woods.[12]

For many who visit the castle today, it is, in part at least, a monument to Gillette's eccentricity, or his inventiveness. It was no sudden manifestation, for in 1907, Rennold Wolf found in the Hartford Gillette house "unique pieces of furniture, bizarre book cases, queer picture frames, marvellous tables and chairs".[5]

About some of the trivia of living, Gillette showed himself more than normally meticulous. Ward Morehouse received from him, in anticipation of a visit to the castle, "a two-page letter, giving directions in elaborate detail and . . . a map in red ink and black, that must have taken half an hour's time . . .".[13] The Parker House, famed hostelry in Boston, received a letter from Gillette in 1929 asking that his favorite suite be reserved, and including a detailed diagram "in red ink and black", indicating exactly what he wanted in the way of accommodations.[14] When Gillette ordered carpets for the castle, his letters to Joseph Marcus, formerly of the rug and carpet department at G. Fox and Co. in Hartford, gave measurements to the half-inch, and exact colors. Mr. Marcus recalled, however, that Mr. Gillette was a charming man to visit, and in his own words: "He was the most wonderful man to deal with; he was a gentleman."[15]

Gillette, gentleman though he was, *could* lose his reserve and restraint. According to Ward Morehouse, he was "a star who never forgot his manners and seldom lost his temper. He did lose it completely, however, near the close of a performance of *Secret Service*. He was delivering his big, final-act speech when an actor playing a Confederate soldier sneezed and a gigantic sneeze it was. Nearly every player on the crowded stage broke up; they all turned from the audience, but shaking shoulders were beyond their control. When the curtain fell, Gillette was white with rage. He glared at his company and spoke in a low voice: 'You people have no right to stand on this side of the curtain. You are only useful out front. That's where you belong'. He turned and walked away."[16]

Charles Frohman thought Gillette was "near", a euphemism for parsimonious, a quality which seems to have amused the great producer and close friend of Gillette. Ward Morehouse wrote that "on one occasion, during a trans-Atlantic voyage early in the century, Jessie Busley, a member of his [Frohman's] company, had a headache, and Gillette gave her two powders. In telling Frohman that her headache was relieved, Miss Busley said: 'Willie G. gave me two headache powders.' And then, Frohman, with a twinkle, said simply, 'Not two!'." But there was also the story of "Matches Mary" who used to peddle her matches outside the New York theatres. During Gillette's revival season at the Empire in December of 1910—he was doing five of his famous plays—he invited Mary and her family to occupy a box for the Christmas Eve performance of "Secret Service". Mary's party had the box bulging with humanity of all ages and sizes, and after the performance, Gillette entertained his guests with refreshments backstage. There were tears in the eyes of Matches Mary when the evening was over and in her hand was her host's check for one hundred dollars.[16]

Rennold Wolf gave a clue to Gillette's kind of generosity when he wrote: "To the worthy in need, he is the cream of human kindness . . . but his beneficence must remain a secret."[5] His many generosities and kindnesses to relatives were presumably "secrets", except to the recipients. The episode of the Yeamans benefit tickets is also revealing of Gillette characteristics. In November 1902, Gillette received by mail two tickets for a benefit performance for a Mrs. Yeamans, veteran comedienne who was celebrating her sixty-seventh birthday and the fifty-seventh anniversary of her first stage appearance. He returned the tickets without comment, and when asked whether he had anything to say, replied, "The story is quite correct." The *New York Tribune* reported what it called this "rather unpleasant episode" in its November 16 issue, stating that the incident had come to the knowledge of Broadway the day before and had been much discussed. The story went on: "Mr. Gillette was spoken of in rather harsh terms by many when the facts became known. Just why Mr. Gillette has not a perfect right to return the tickets which he did not solicit is almost as hard to understand, however, as is the motive which would profit those who alone knew the facts to make the story public."

A similar reaction was felt on Broadway when the provisions of Gillette's will were made public and it became known that he had remembered only his relatives and close personal associates. The *New York Daily News* of May 5, 1937 took a somewhat chiding tone in reporting that Gillette had left nothing to the charities of his profession or to any of the organizations such as the Players and the Lambs Club, in which he took a friendly interest during his lifetime. His chief concern seemed to be the fate of his castle. The facts of the will were that if the residuary legatees died, then five charitable institutions were to inherit, namely, the Connecticut Children's Aid Society, the Actors' Fund of America, the Bide-a-Wee Home (for pets) in New York City, the Connecticut Humane Society in Hartford, and the Seabury Memorial Home in New York City.

Stories of escapism notwithstanding, Gillette, for most of his life, was far from a recluse. Billie Burke wrote that he was "full of fun".[4] He aided and abetted Charles Frohman in some of his practical jokes. Maude Adams related that Frohman loved to play tricks, and William Gillette was an able helper. The year of what Maude referred to as "the new lights", Mr. Gillette had begun performances at the Empire. He had had one of his usual successes, and needed to prolong his stay in New York. Barrie plays had first place at the Empire, and Maude went in for rehearsals with her Barrie play; this was a pleasant situation, since there she had her "lamps". Gillette moved his play to the Garrick, but he and Frohman connived, and when the play was transferred, the lights went, too. Maude had to endure two dress rehearsals without her "lamps". They did come back, however, for the first night, as she had known they would.[17]

Although a reserved New Englander, Gillette nevertheless liked the company of ladies, particularly young ones, and was not above gestures of gallantry. John Barrymore's biographer wrote that Ethel Barrymore, as a young woman, was long an admirer of Gillette. He continued: "Ethel, introduced to Gillette, found him charming indeed. But entirely unknown to himself, the alumnus of four cap-and-gown factories shattered the girl's illusions. He held Ethel's hand a moment too long."[18] Billie Burke spoke of Will as a "gay and gallant gentleman who, it seemed, was always returning from Kissington, his cue to kiss your shoulder".[4] He was reported married or engaged to nearly all of his leading ladies,[19] but remained faithful to the memory of Helen.

His wit and humor have been variously described as "searching" and "blade-like".[20] Billie Burke gave an example of the wit, "capable of more searching thrusts . . . than what passes for repartee in today's tedious cafe society. Once he was discussing a middle-aging actor who had married a young wife. 'Yes', he said, 'poor-so-and-so, he has a young wife who loves him passionately and annoys him in other ways.' "[4]

William Lyon Phelps thought that Gillette was continually amused and entertained by his own mind.[21] At the time of Gillette's death, Phelps wrote in the *New Haven Register* that Gillette was "one of the most original and witty letter writers [he] ever knew".

His playfully testy letters are perhaps even better examples of his kind of humor than the Billie Burke story. Writing to Alexander Woollcott concerning difficulties over the spelling of one's name, he said: "What you want to do—if you don't mind a little advice—is to get some damned inventor to associate your name with a razor. I had a lot of trouble with my final e until Gillette came along with his face-lacerator, after which all was well."[22] And to Brander Matthews, in returning the galley proof of an introduction he had written for Matthews, Gillette complained: "I find proof emanating from under your control most trying to deal with, for it is impossible to know whether the things are bungling errors proceeding from ignorant bums from Mott Street who have tried to set type while intoxicated, or are the results of those new rules for spelling with which you appear to be obsessed."[23]

The *National Cyclopedia of American Biography* states that one of Will's friends described him as "a boy at heart", fond of the outdoors, nature, and children. To these, cats should be added, for they were one of Gillette's favorite diversions. He often had or found one when he was on tour, took one or more on the "Aunt Polly", and is credited with having had fifteen or more at the castle. Readers of the *Deep River New Era* one day found in their papers the following advertisement: "Two perfectly black Tommy Kittens to be given away. One all black, other black with white feet and underside. Both have double fore-paws—that is, seven-toed. Not Persian, Angora, or Siamese, but real cats. They come of a family of great mousers. Anyone wanting one or both of these delightful felines, must write stating qualifications—that is, we want to be sure that they do not go to stupid boobs who don't know what a cat is. Would like to have recommendation from last cats you have lived with, but probably that is asking too much. Address WG, Box 96, Hadlyme, Ct."

His letters to relatives and close friends are most revealing of the inner Gillette—his whimsical, sometimes bizarre, humor, his charm and affection, and his humanness, including feelings of loneliness and pessimism. Sophie, his brother Ed's wife, was the confidante of his homesickness when he first went West at twenty. He wrote Sophie and Ed in 1886, when his career was turning successful, that he was twenty or thirty years older than when he had seen them last. He told Sophie in 1893 that, although he wanted to be with his mother as much as possible, he did not like it very well in Hartford. Later he expressed the pessimism that had come to be a part of him since Helen's death: "There is a sort of rest in knowing of how little consequence anything is." To "Dr." Fuller and to Sophie, he expressed his feelings of loneliness, writing to the "Dr." in February 1894: "Say—why can't some of you fellows adopt me—I'm awfully alone", and to Sophie in April 1894 he wrote: "I long to be with you for I have no home no dear ones indeed but you [meaning Sophie and his two nieces] —and the clouds are heavy about me—my chief consolation is that life is worth nothing *anyway*—so an end to anxiety about it."[24]

The need to care about others and to have them care about him remained throughout his life. In 1912 he wrote from Germany to his niece "Ivey", Sophie's younger daughter, that he needed to have her miss him. Gillette's own mind, as William Lyon Phelps suggested, was probably his salvation. By the mid and late 1890's, he seems to have been genuinely caught up in his theatre world and mature enough to have left behind the worst of pessimism and loneliness, though there were recurrences of his physical ailment. The place he made for himself in the theatre was sustaining, and his close personal relationships were generous, sincere, and likewise supporting. "Dr." Fuller wrote in 1912: "Dear good William Gillette honored me with a ½ hour call yesterday. He is the noblest Roman of them all."

At his death, the *Boston Herald* of April 20, 1937, commented: "Gillette, a gentleman born, gradually created, and scrupulously maintained for nearly 50 years, a reputation for professional and personal integrity." And Clayton Hamilton, at the time of "Three Wise Fools", said of him: "He was esteemed not merely for his present powers but also in affectionate remembrance of his more than half a century of service as a dramatist, a brilliant actor, and an imaginative stage director. As the sole active survivor of the many giants of the golden age of acting, he seemed to sum up in himself a sort of national nostalgia for the good old days of the theatre, when the playhouse appeared as an enchanted realm of glamour and splendor and imaginative fascination."[25]

William Gillette devoted himself to the theatre for most of his eighty-three years. His personality, plays, and acting were a unique contribution to American life and to the stage of his time. Those who experienced his creations found in them delight and memories to be cherished.

Notes

CHAPTER I

1. Doris E. Cook, "The Library of William Gillette" in *Bulletin of Bibliography,* XXII, Sept.–Dec. 1957, 89.
2. *New York Times,* Nov. 1, 1914, V.
3. "Hail Columbia" file in the Connecticut State Library.
4. Billy Garvie, "Early Hartford Theatres" (Paper and newspaper clippings in The Connecticut Historical Society).
5. *Hartford Courant,* March 6, 1873.
6. Hooker Letters, Stowe-Day Foundation, Hartford.
7. Cornelia Otis Skinner, *Family Circle* (Boston: Houghton, Mifflin, 1948), 55.
8. Collection of the H. P. H. S. Report Cards of Lucy S. Williams at The Connecticut Historical Society.
9. *New York Times,* Nov. 1, 1914, V.
10. *Hartford Courant,* Dec. 6, 1873.
11. Doris E. Cook, "The Library of William Gillette" in *Bulletin of Bibliography,* XXII, Jan.–Apr. 1958, 120.
12. Otis Skinner, *Footlights and Spotlights* (Indianapolis: Bobbs-Merrill Co., Inc., c.1924, R.1951), 21. Reprinted by permission of the publishers.
13. *Hartford Times,* Jan. 10, 1872.
14. Advertising poster in newspaper portion of Elizabeth Ives Gillette collection, Stowe-Day Foundation, Hartford.
15. Glen Hughes, *The Story of the Theatre* (N.Y. and Lond.: S. French, 1928), 235.

CHAPTER II

1. Richard Burton, "William Gillette—an American Playwright" in *The Book Buyer,* Feb. 1898.
2. Edward Hooker, *The Descendants of Rev. Thomas Hooker* (Rochester, 1909).
3. Letters of Gillette to his sister-in-law, Sophie Stoddard Gillette, at the Research Library of the Stowe-Day Foundation, Hartford, confirm Gillette's presence in St. Louis in September and October 1873, and in New Orleans in November 1873.

4. Clippings in William Gillette material, New York Public Library at Lincoln Center, New York City.
5. *New York Times,* Nov. 1, 1914, V.
6. Albert Bigelow Paine, *A Short Life of Mark Twain* (Garden City: Garden City Pub. Co., 1920), 161–162.
7. *Hartford Courant,* Jan. 11, 1875.
8. *Hartford Courant,* Jan. 12, 1875.
9. Albert Bigelow Paine, *Mark Twain, a Biography* (N.Y. & Lond.: Harper, 1912), I, 539.
10. Joseph Hopkins Twichell, Manuscript journal, May 7, 1875. Joseph Hopkins Twichell Collection, Collection of American Literature, Yale University Library.
11. *Hartford Courant,* May 7, 1875.
12. *Boston Evening Transcript,* Feb. 3, 1876.
13. Inquiries at the colleges mentioned in various unauthorized biographical sketches of Gillette have failed to produce evidence of any other truly formal education.
14. *Boston University Year Book,* 1875–76, 112–113.
15. Information from prompt copies of plays in Gillette's library listed in "The Library of William Gillette" in *Bulletin of Bibliography,* XXII, Sept. 1957–Aug. 1958.
16. *Hartford Courant,* June 6, 1877.
17. *Hartford Times,* Oct. 20, 1879.

CHAPTER III

1. *Hartford Courant,* Jan. 9, 1880.
2. *Hartford Courant,* Jan. 10, 1880.
3. *Hartford Evening Post,* Jan. 10, 1880.
4. Gillette letter, Jan. 1880, in Twichell Journal, Joseph Hopkins Twichell Collection, Collection of American Literature, Yale University Library. The "evils" of the theatre were real to people even after the eighties. See Guthrie McClintic's *Me and Kit,* (Boston, 1955), 18; when *his* father found out about his secret matinee excursions, he said he would see his son "burn in hell-fire before he would let him hang around a lot of God-damned pimps and whores".

5. Joseph Hopkins Twichell. Manuscript journal, Jan. 11, 1880, Joseph Hopkins Twichell Collection, Collection of American Literature, Yale University Library.
6. Warner letters, Stowe-Day Foundation, Hartford.
7. Annie E. Trumbull scrapbook in The Connecticut Historical Society.
8. Peter Clark Macfarlane, "The Magic of William Gillette" in *Everybody's Magazine,* Feb. 1915, 262.
9. Percy MacKaye, *Epoch: The Life of Steel MacKaye* (N.Y.: Boni & Liveright, 1927), I, 373.
10. *New York Times,* June 2, 1881.
11. *Boston Evening Transcript,* Mar. 21, 1882.
12. Guthrie Burton, *Three Parts Scotch, an Informal Autobiography* (Indianapolis, N.Y.: Bobbs-Merrill Co., Inc., c.1946), 147. Used with permission of the publishers.
13. *Hartford Courant,* Dec. 16, 1884.
14. *Hartford Courant,* May 29, 1883.
15. *New York Times,* Sept. 30, 1884.
16. Brown Dramatic Scrapbooks, Boston Public Library, Vol. 15, 38, and Peter Clark Macfarlane, "The Magic of William Gillette", *Everybody's Magazine,* Feb. 1915.
17. Gillette letters, Stowe-Day Foundation, Hartford.
18. *Hartford Times,* Dec. 12, 1884.
19. *Hartford Courant,* Mar. 17, 1886.
20. Roberts Opera House Record Book, The Connecticut Historical Society.
21. Eugene Tompkins, *History of the Boston Theatre, 1854–1901* (Bost. & N.Y.: Houghton Mifflin, 1908), 318–319.
22. Warner letters, Stowe-Day Foundation, Hartford.
23. *New York Times,* Aug. 16, 1886.
24. *Boston Evening Transcript,* Dec. 28, 1886.
25. *Hartford Courant,* Oct. 17, 1919.
26. Gillette letters, Stowe-Day Foundation, Hartford.
27. Isaac F. Marcosson and Daniel Frohman, *Charles Frohman: Manager and Man* (N.Y. and Lond.: Harper, 1916), 114–115.
28. *New York Tribune,* Nov. 30, 1887.
29. *New York Times,* Aug. 15, 1888.
30. The Greenwich, Conn., vital statistics records list peritonitis as the cause of death.

CHAPTER IV

1. Gillette-Fuller letters, The Connecticut Historical Society.
2. Gillette letters, Stowe-Day Foundation, Hartford.
3. Warner letters, Stowe-Day Foundation, Hartford.
4. *Boston Evening Transcript,* Mar. 4, 1890.
5. *New York Times,* Sept. 8, 1890.
6. Frank P. Morse, *Backstage with Henry Miller.* Copyright, 1938 by E. P. Dutton & Co., Inc., N.Y. Renewal, ©, 1966 by Frank P. Morse, 175–177. Published by E. P. Dutton & Co., Inc. and used with their permission.
7. Hooker letters, Stowe-Day Foundation, Hartford.
8. *New York Times,* Mar. 31, 1891.
9. *New York Times,* Feb. 7, 1893.
10. Letter to "Dr." Fuller, James Keddie, Jr., Collection, Wellesley Hills, Mass.
11. Beecher Family Letters, Schlesinger Library, Radcliffe College.

CHAPTER V

1. Gertrude Lynch, "The Real William Gillette" in *Theatre,* XIII, Apr. 1911, 124.
2. Gillette-Fuller letters at The Connecticut Historical Society.
3. *Boston Sunday Herald,* Mar. 3, 1901.
4. Isaac F. Marcosson and Daniel Frohman, *Charles Frohman: Manager and Man* (N.Y. and Lond.: Harper, 1916), 114–115.
5. *Ibid.,* 117.
6. Cornelia Otis Skinner, *Family Circle* (Bost.: Houghton, Mifflin, 1948), 143–144.
7. From *Mrs. Fiske and the American Theatre,* by Archie Binns, p. 56. © 1955 by Archie Binns. Used by permission of Crown Publishers, Inc.
8. Marcosson and Frohman, *op. cit.,* 156–157.
9. *New York Times,* Nov. 27, 1894.
10. *New Yorker,* Jan. 25, 1964.
11. *New York Times,* Jan. 16, 1964.
12. *New York Herald Tribune,* Jan. 1964.
13. Marcosson and Frohman, *op. cit.,* 196–197.

Notes

14. Walter Pritchard Eaton, "Life Begins Again at 80 for Actor William Gillette", *Boston Herald,* Feb. 2, 1936.
15. Gene Fowler, *Good Night, Sweet Prince* (N.Y.: Viking, 1944), 81.
16. *New York Times,* Oct. 6, 1896.
17. Marcosson and Frohman, *op. cit.,* 197.
18. P. M. Stone, "William Gillette's Stage Career" in *The Baker Street Journal,* Vol. 12, No. 1, New Series, 1962, 12.
19. Barbara Marinarci, *Leading Ladies* (N.Y.: Dodd, Mead & Co., 1961), 220.
20. P. M. Stone, *op. cit.,* 12.
21. George Bernard Shaw, *Plays and Players* (Lond., N.Y.: Oxford, 1955), 239–240. Reprinted by permission of The Public Trustee and The Society of Authors.
22. Gertrude Stein, *Lectures in America* (N.Y.: Random House, Inc., c.1935), 116–117.
23. *New York Tribune,* Aug. 15, 1897.
24. P. M. Stone, *op. cit.,* 12–13.
25. Marcosson and Frohman, *op. cit.,* 235.
26. Gillette-Watson letters, Connecticut State Library.

CHAPTER VI

1. *Hartford Courant,* Mar. 22, 1898.
2. Gillette-Russell letters, Manuscript Division, New York Public Library.
3. Gillette-Fuller letters, The Connecticut Historical Society.
4. *Hartford Courant,* July 19, 1953.
5. *Des Moines Register,* Sept. 4, 1910.
6. Gillette-Watson letters, Connecticut State Library.
7. Rennold Wolf, article on Gillette, *Smith's Magazine,* June 1907.
8. Gillette letter to W. G. Postance, Sept. 30, 1929, in George C. Tyler Papers, Princeton University Library.
9. John Dickson Carr, *The Life of Sir Arthur Conan Doyle* (N.Y.: Harper, 1949), 117–118.
10. Harold J. Shepstone, "Mr. Gillette as Sherlock Holmes" in *Strand Magazine,* Dec. 1901.
11. Lewis C. Strang, *Famous Actors of the Day in America* (Bost.: L. C. Page, 1900), 188–189.

12. Annie E. Trumbull Papers, The Connecticut Historical Society.
13. *Hartford Courant,* Mar. 17, 1889.
14. Carr, *op. cit.,* 118.
15. *New York Tribune,* June 25, 1889.
16. *New York Times,* Nov. 7, 1899.
17. *New York Times,* Oct. 17, 1915.
18. Elmer Rice, *The Living Theatre* (N.Y.: Harper, 1959), 18.
19. Frederic Dorr Steele, "Reminiscent Notes", prefatory to 1935 edition of "Sherlock Holmes", Doubleday, Doran & Co., xxvii–xxviii. Mr. Steele's initial remark refers, of course, to the stage character of Sherlock Holmes and not to Sir Arthur Conan Doyle's literary creation.
20. *Hartford Courant,* Oct. 26, 1900.
21. *Hartford Courant,* Dec. 4, 1900.
22. Carr, *op. cit.,* 148.
23. Sir Arthur Conan Doyle, *Memories and Adventures* (Bost.: Little, Brown, 1924), 97.
24. Newspaper clipping, Gillette material, New York Public Library at Lincoln Center.
25. Gillette letters, Stowe-Day Foundation, Hartford.
26. Sir Arthur Conan Doyle to William Gillette. Undated letter in the possession of Horace R. Whittier, Bristol, Conn., quoted in article by Herbert J. Stoeckel, "The Case of Sherlock Holmes", in *Hartford Courant Magazine,* Apr. 11, 1965, p. 8.

CHAPTER VII

1. Otis Skinner, *Footlights and Spotlights* (Indianapolis: Bobbs-Merrill Co., Inc., c.1924, R. 1951), 237. Reprinted by permission of the publishers.
2. 1918 Boston newspaper clipping in Theatre Collection, Harvard College Library.
3. Gillette letters in Connecticut State Library.
4. *New York Times,* Nov. 18, 1903.
5. Max Beerbohm, *Around Theatres* (N.Y.: Knopf, 1930), II, 500, 504.
6. Charles Chaplin, *My Autobiography* (N.Y.: Simon & Schuster, 1964), 88–89. Reprinted by permission of Mr. Chaplin and The Bodley Head, London.

Notes

7. Letter in Gillette material, Theatre Collection, Museum of the City of New York.
8. *Boston Evening Transcript,* Dec. 26, 1905.
9. *Boston Globe,* Dec. 26, 1905.
10. *Hartford Courant,* Feb. 10, 1906.
11. *New York Times,* Oct. 17, 1906.
12. *New York Times,* Oct. 20. 1908.
13. Gertrude Lynch, "The Real William Gillette" in *Theatre,* XIII, 1911, 123.
14. Newspaper clipping in Gillette material, Theatre Collection, Harvard College Library.

CHAPTER VIII

1. Mark Sullivan, *Education of an American* (N.Y.: Doubleday, Doran & Co., 1938), 284.
2. Gillette-Sullivan letters in the possession of Mrs. Jameson Parker, daughter of Mark Sullivan, Gunston Hall, Lorton, Virginia.
3. *New York Times,* Mar. 15, 1913.
4. Vincent Starrett, *Born in a Bookshop: Chapters from the Chicago Renascence* (Norman: University of Oklahoma Press, c.1965), 122–123.
5. Charles W. Burpee, "Hartford's Literary Colony in the Heart of Nook Farm", in *Hartford Courant,* May 1, 1921, III.
6. William Gillette. Letter on display in upper room at Gillette Castle.
7. Gillette letters to Hamlin Garland, University of Southern California Library.
8. *New York Times,* Aug. 23, 1914.
9. Guthrie McClintic, *Me and Kit* (Bost.: Little, Brown, 1955), 136–137.
10. *New York Times,* Oct. 21, 1914.
11. *Hartford Courant,* May 8, 1915.
12. *New York Times,* Nov. 1, 1914, V.
13. *Hartford Courant,* Oct. 17, 1919.
14. Otis Skinner, *Footlights and Spotlights* (Indianapolis: Bobbs-Merrill Co., Inc., c.1924, R.1951), 287–288. Reprinted by permission of the publishers.
15. Gillette letter, Nov. 30, 1915, to Ripley Hitchcock, Hitchcock Collection, Columbia University Libraries.

16. Gillette letter, Aug. 14, 1916, to Brander Matthews, Special Manuscript Collections, Columbia University Libraries.
17. *New York Times,* Feb. 6, 1917.
18. Catherine H. Burns, *Letters to Mary* (N.Y.: Random House, Inc., c.1940), 83–85, 115, 117, 119–123, 127–133. This and previous and following quotes on "Dear Brutus".
19. *New York Times,* Dec. 24, 1918.
20. Gillette letter to Mr. Johnson, July 1, 1918, American Academy of Arts and Letters.
21. Gillette letter to "Alf" in James Keddie, Jr., Collection, Wellesley Hills, Mass.
22. "Dear Brutus" programs in the Library and Museum of the Performing Arts at Lincoln Center and in the James Keddie, Jr., Collection, Wellesley Hills, Mass.
23. *New York Times,* Nov. 22, 1921.
24. *New York Times,* Mar. 26, 1922.
25. *New York Times,* Apr. 19, 1923.
26. *New York Times,* Sept. 7, 1924.
27. Gillette-Watson letters, Connecticut State Library.
28. Gillette letter to Alexander Woollcott, Harvard Theatre Collection. By permission of the Harvard College Library.
29. *Hartford Courant,* Sept. 17, 1918.

CHAPTER IX

1. Gillette-Watson letters, Connecticut State Library.
2. Gillette letters to George Crouse Tyler, Princeton University Library. This and all subsequent Tyler references.
3. *New York Times,* Aug. 13, 1929.
4. *New York Times,* Nov. 18, 1929.
5. Ward Morehouse, *Matinee Tomorrow* (N.Y., Lond., Toronto: Whittlesey House, 1949), 230–231.
6. *New York Times,* Nov. 26, 1929.
7. *Hartford Courant,* Feb. 11, 1930.
8. *Hartford Courant,* Apr. 30, 1937.
9. *New York Times,* May 13, 1930.
10. *New York Times,* Oct. 26, 1930, IX.

11. *New York Times,* Nov. 12, 1931.
12. *Boston Transcript,* Dec. 3, 1931 (clipping in New York Public Library Theatre Collection).
13. Gillette letter to Eleanor Robson Belmont in Belmont Collection, Columbia University Libraries.
14. Guthrie Burton, *Three Parts Scotch, an Informal Autobiography* (Indianapolis, N.Y., Bobbs-Merrill Co., Inc. c.1946), 153–156, 162. Used by permission of the publishers.
15. *Hartford Times,* July 24, 1933.
16. Gillette letter to Alexander Woollcott, Harvard Theatre Collection. By permission of the Harvard College Library.
17. Vincent Starrett, *Born in a Bookshop: Chapters from the Chicago Renascence* (Norman: University of Oklahoma Press, c.1965), 280–281.
18. Gillette letter to Perriton Maxwell, Brooklyn Public Library.
19. Ward Morehouse, "Broadway After Dark", in *New York Sun,* Oct. 5, 1935.
20. *New York Times,* Nov. 24, 1935, IX.
21. *Hartford Courant,* Apr. 20, 1937.
22. Henry A. Perkins, Address at the Opening of Gillette Castle, in *Connecticut Woodlands,* Vol. 10, No. 1, Feb. 1945.

CHAPTER X

1. Mary Lawton, *A Lifetime with Mark Twain* (N.Y.: Harcourt Brace, 1925), 25.
2. Leo Carroll letter to P. M. Stone in James Keddie, Jr., Collection, Wellesley Hills, Mass.
3. Picture in Gillette scrapbook at Connecticut State Library.
4. Billie Burke, *With a Feather on My Nose* (N.Y.: Appleton-Century-Crofts, 1948), 53, 69.
5. Rennold Wolf article on Gillette in *Smith's Magazine,* June 1907.
6. Ward Morehouse, "The Hadlyme Notables" in *New York Sun,* Feb. 29, 1936.
7. Daniel Frohman, *Daniel Frohman Presents, an Autobiography* (N.Y.: Kendall & Sharp, 1935), 52.
8. Henry A. Perkins, "William Gillette, the Man", in *Connecticut Woodlands,* Vol. 10, No. 1, Feb. 1945.

9. *New York Times,* July 24, 1935.
10. W. H. Briggs letter to Gillette, May 2, 1928, Pierpont Morgan Library.
11. Amy Leslie in *Chicago Daily News,* Oct. 9, 1897—clipping at Stowe-Day Foundation, Hartford.
12. Alice Hamilton, *Exploring the Dangerous Trades: Autobiography* (Bost.: Atlantic-Little, Brown, and Co., 1943), 410.
13. Ward Morehouse, "Broadway after Dark" in *New York Sun,* Oct. 5, 1935.
14. *The Baker Street Journal,* XII, No. 1, 1962.
15. Bill Ryan, *Hartford Times* column on Gillette letters.
16. Ward Morehouse, *Matinee Tomorrow* (N.Y., Lond.: Whittlesey House, 1949), 22–23.
17. Phyllis Robbins, *Maude Adams, an Intimate Portrait* (N.Y.: Putnam, c.1956), 48.
18. Gene Fowler, *Good Night, Sweet Prince* (N.Y.: Viking, 1944), 82. Fowler's designation "alumnus" is erroneous.
19. Theatrical Biographies, Brown Dramatic Collection, Boston Public Library, Vol. 7, 90.
20. Guthrie Burton, *Three Parts Scotch, an Informal Autobiography* (Indianapolis, N.Y.: Bobbs-Merrill Co., Inc., c.1946), 166.
21. In American Academy of Arts and Letters *Publication* No. 96, 1940.
22. Gillette letter to Alexander Woollcott, Harvard Theatre Collection. By permission of the Harvard College Library.
23. Gillette to Brander Matthews, Special Manuscript Collections, Columbia University Libraries.
24. Gillette letters at Stowe-Day Foundation, Hartford, and "Dr." Fuller letters at The Connecticut Historical Society.
25. *New York Post,* Feb. 2, 1936.